MW00637296

CHOOSE WISELY

A 31 DAY DEVOTIONAL

Learn How to Make Choices
To Transform Your Life

Choose Wisely

A 31 Day Devotional

Learn How to Make Choices
To Transform Your Life

Debby Sibert

A Note from the Author:

It is my passion to help people discover their life's purpose and experience the blessings of God by intentionally making wise choices, empowering them to unlock their God-given potential. I pray that this devotional series will aid in transformation to that end.

It is my heart's desire that everyone would have an opportunity to meet Jesus—to experience Him intimately, to have their hearts transformed by His love and grace, and to learn the peace, joy, and victory that comes from a "sold-out" life of surrender and obedience. Are you "All In" for Christ?

TABLE OF CONTENTS

INTRODUCTION

You know, we make thousands of choices every day, most of them without thinking. Thankfully many choices can happen on the subconscious level, so we don't have to think about them.

However, some of the choices we make consciously have become habits that don't serve us well. We have to become intentional about avoiding those poor choices to experience a better way of life. Do you desire a deeper walk with Christ? Do you want to make a positive impact and leave the world around you a bit better than you found it? Then let's choose to make wiser decisions remembering that words matter, character counts and our conduct—what we think, say and do reveals our heart.

Are you by any chance feeling a little stuck or in a rut, wanting more satisfaction in life for yourself? The purpose of this 31-day devotional series is to help us all focus on godly characteristics and attributes that can become a daily part of our character and equip us to make wise choices.

Did you realize that we make choices, then our choices make us? Some of our good choices have resulted in a happy marriage, a great job, a deep, personal satisfaction. Some of our poor choices have resulted in destroying a marriage, losing a job, and suffering shame and regret. Few things will determine the quality and fulfillment of our life more than the choices we make - for better or for worse.

Today I want to start this series by briefly discussing the benefits of choosing wisely.

Our goal as a Christ-follower should be to become more like Christ in our thoughts, words, and actions. We are to develop the mind of Christ. Of course, we will never really arrive at that state completely until we meet Him face to face. This is all part of the sanctification process. But since He lives inside of us in the person of the Holy Spirit, we have available to us His character traits and many of His attributes. They could remain dormant, but it should be our desire to live those out in our lives.

When we make wise choices based on God's word, they will bring us the satisfaction in life that we all long for, which will gradually transform our lifestyle into one that will be an example for others and point them to Christ.

So, as difficult as it may seem on the surface to live out some of the qualities and choices we will be discussing over the next 31 days, if you will commit and devote yourself to intentionally incorporate these choices your lifestyle, you will come out of this series a different person.

One of the greatest gifts God gave us was the gift of choice and we are responsible for what we do with that gift. It could be a curse if not handled properly. God doesn't force anything on us. Our life experiences are based pretty much on our choices and the consequences of them. Think about it—sin entered our world because of one poor choice. We need God's wisdom which we will discuss later on.

My goal in this series is to help you fall in love with Jesus in a new and fresh way as we discuss all these character qualities that He modeled for us in the Scriptures. As we focus our attention on His attributes and embrace an eternal perspective, imitating what He modeled for us, the more we will think and act like Him. Isn't that awesome? And isn't that what you want? We become like those with whom we spend the most time. By engaging in this series, I hope we will learn how or increase our ability to:

1. Live intentionally so that the choices we make will lead to positive results and influence in our lives and the lives of others.

2. Avoid poor choices when a quick decision is necessary. We'll know how to respond in a Christ-like way.

3. Discover the truth and clarity behind our choices.

4. Appreciate how our choices will foster close relationships and heal division by choosing thoughtful words and actions.

5. Understand the "why" behind our choices so we can move forward with positivity in all areas of our life.

6. Consider the long-term impact of our choices so that we intentionally leave an eternal legacy that points others to Christ.

7. Recognize any red flags of obstacles to our living a Christ-like life that otherwise could result in future regrets.

I have chosen one word or keyword phrase per day for the next 31 days for us to focus on as a choice for that day. You will find some "crossover" in some of these traits and attributes. Just like all things work together for good for those who love Him and are called according to His purpose (Romans 8:28), all these attributes are intertwined to help mold you into who God wants you to be. Hopefully, they will meld into your total being, defining whose you are.

It's so easy in life to live on autopilot rather than to live intentionally. We often sabotage ourselves with our negative thoughts and limiting beliefs, so we need to change our way of thinking. We need to change our choices. I can relate so well to this!

The way we think affects how we feel, and how we feel affects the way we behave. If we want to change the way we act, we must go back and change our thoughts and choices. If you are feeling angry, for example, it's because you are choosing angry thoughts. We can't change our feelings, but we can change our thoughts that are creating those feelings.

The choices I have selected for this series are many of the ones God has been weaving into my life over these many years of being a Christ-follower. I have to say, they have been transformative, and I pray they will be for you as well. I still have to live every day with intentionality. That never ends, but over time it becomes a way of life. Remember, life is a journey. Give yourself grace as you go through this.

Please come back to each day periodically to see how you are doing on that particular "life choice." If any of this is going to be helpful, it must involve action. Head knowledge is not enough. There has to be a habitual application for change to take place. It will take a good month or two of daily intentionality for new habits to form, but it will be well worth it. Whenever we want to get rid of an old habit or choice, we need to replace it with a new/better one. In changing our focus (our choices), we rewire our hearts and experience a transformed mind.

I have tried to keep each devotional to be short and to the point. While every choice God has given me to share is significant, I have started

Jesus chose to die for us. The least we can do is to choose to live for Him.

with one of THE most important choices we should begin with every day. So, tomorrow we will discuss "Gratitude." Pray today that the Lord would prepare your heart to receive and be willing to put into practice all these amazing attributes we will be discussing in your life daily.

We are only as close to God as we choose to be. Keep in mind, God gives us the freedom to make choices; however,

4

we have to deal with, and don't get to choose the consequences of both the good and bad choices we make.

Jesus *chose* to die for us. The least we can do is to *choose* to live for Him.

Live honorably, love completely, and choose wisely. Make wise choices today. God bless, and I'll see you tomorrow.

Ephesians 5:20
1 Thes 5:16-18

DAY 1
Choose Gratitude

I'm a slow learner about many essential things in life, but I work very hard to make them a way of life when I do learn them. One of the most important lessons I've learned is the benefit of developing an attitude of gratitude. It benefits not only me but everyone around me.

I've learned that gratitude is the "breakthrough" attitude. The more grateful I am, the more breakthroughs I seem to have in life. One thing I consistently try to do, which has served me well, is to intentionally give thanks in all things knowing that God is sovereign. He is in control, His plan is perfect and He has my back. It can't get much better than that!

Are you a glass half full or a glass half empty sort of person? Do you find yourself being negative or anxious about things? While anxiety can partially be genetically predisposed and could be a clinical issue for some, it is generally an ingrained learned habit we can unlearn with the correct practices. Anxiety focuses on negativity and limiting beliefs that can be counteracted by practicing gratitude regarding those things you are genuinely grateful for, no matter how small or insignificant they may seem.

You know, as Christ-followers, we have so much for which to be grateful. If you are in the midst of a trying time right now, remember that God never promised us smooth sailing. Still, He does promise that He will be right there with us, restoring us and urging us onward. He is there to fill us up so we can continue to fill others.

Eventually, if you make it a practice to look, you will find more and more things you are grateful for until you develop an overall attitude of gratitude. This changes neuropathways, causing a rewiring of your brain from negativity to positivity. Neuroscience has proven this to be effective in literally changing our brain's default position. This is a very simplistic explanation of an actual complex but valuable and well-documented process of how we can change our brains.

Neurologist Dr. David Perlmutter says, "From the medical perspective, there is healing that is activated when we practice gratitude. High levels of stress activate cortisol in our brains, specifically our hippocampus, which controls our mood." He says that "The best way to change our neurochemistry, elevate our mood, and decrease the amount of cortisol in our body, is to elevate the corners of our mouth. All we have to do to lower the cortisol, the stress in our body is to smile." That's easy to do when practicing gratitude.

Did you know, or ever even think about the fact that you cannot be disgruntled and grateful at the same time? It's true, and science has proved that your brain will not allow it, so you have to choose. Are you going to be grumpy or grateful? It's simply a choice— you are in control. You decide. You choose. Now, suppose this doesn't come naturally, which, unless that is already your natural mindset and bent, you may very well have to ask the Lord to help you with that. In that case, you can be very sure He will be quick and grateful to answer that prayer.

The grateful heart is much like a magnet sweeping over the day, collecting reasons to be thankful.

It is amazing how our life can change when we make gratitude for what we do have our focus. It creates a heart change that can overcome any adversity. Only Christ can give us what we need to overcome any difficult circumstances in life. Unbelievers, and even we Christians, tend to think that getting "things" and "solutions" will bring contentment. The only problem is that when the goal is achieved, I'm sure you have discovered, it usually doesn't deliver the expected gratification. Maybe initially, but it doesn't last.

What is your attitude? Is it one of gratitude? We are told when we stop to count our blessings, they seem to multiply exponentially. Conversely, if we look at all the things we don't have, it will appear that we never have enough. A grateful heart sees each day as a gift, and thankful people focus less on what they lack and more on the privileges they have. The grateful heart is much like a magnet sweeping over the day, collecting reasons to be thankful.

To quote Max Lucado from his blog:

"Gratitude gets us through the hard stuff. To reflect on your blessings is to rehearse God's accomplishments. To rehearse God's accomplishments is to discover His heart. To discover His heart is to discover not just good gifts but the Good Giver. Gratitude always leaves us looking at God and away from dread. It does to anxiety what the morning sun does to valley mist. It burns it up."

There are so many Scripture verses that speak to this, but I will leave you with two. First, from Ephesians 5:20, "Giving thanks always and for everything to God the Father in the name of our Lord Jesus Christ." And this one from 1 Thessalonians 5:16-18: "Rejoice always, pray without ceasing, give thanks in all circumstances; for this is the will of God in Christ Jesus for you."

Let me ask you this: What if you wake up tomorrow with only the things you thanked God for today? When I first stumbled across that question, it stopped me dead in my tracks. *Would I wake up with anything?* It's a humbling and provocative idea.

I don't ask this question to make you feel guilty or coerce you to list every single blessing every day painstakingly. It's simply a good reminder to keep gratitude at the forefront of our minds—to intentionally thank the Lord for all the gifts He gives us.

Especially if you don't believe that a simple daily attitude change can significantly change your life, I challenge you to intentionally put this to a test for the next month at least, until it becomes a lifestyle habit. Today's call to action, from now on, is to start your day before you even get out of bed, thinking about and thanking God for several things for which you are grateful.

Live honorably, love completely, and choose wisely - choose to have an attitude of gratitude today. God bless, and I'll see you tomorrow!

My marriage
my many strong relationships +
friendships!
Sun Valley our house + hiking
all over.
For my Oreo
For freedom from responsibilities.

1 John 3:18

DAY 2
Choose Love

Let's talk about love. It's not just the first fruit mentioned in the fruit of the spirit. It is *the* fruit. All of the others, which we will discuss later in later devotions, are simply expressions of the fruit of love. Love is a very misunderstood word because it's so often misused. We say we love our spouse, but we also save we love pizza and ice cream, our dog, and to sleep in on a Saturday morning.

In the English language, we use the same word, "love," to mean many different things. We also seem to think that love is something we can't control. We say things like, "I fell 'in' or 'out' of love" when, in fact, the Bible tells us that love is not only controllable but also a matter of conduct. 1 John 3:18 tells us, "Little children, let us not love in word or talk but in deed and in truth." Love is a verb, and it's a decision, not just a feeling.

Jesus commands that we love others. Love is a choice, an action. In Colossians 3:14, Paul tells us to put on love as if it were a garment. Since love is a choice, it's also controllable. For us to know how to love, we first need to experience God's love for ourselves. We can't give what we don't have.

Suppose you find yourself having a difficult time loving others. In that case, you probably feel unloved by someone based on something that happened in your past. It's impossible to love others fully and completely

11

while at the same time resenting someone else. So we can't love God, who we cannot see fully, while holding resentments toward someone else we can see. A divided heart cannot love unconditionally, and a bitter heart is a divided heart.

So how do we take on a loving heart—a loving spirit? We do this by taking the focus off ourselves and putting it on to other people's needs, hurts, problems, etc. You may have noticed that the most unlovable and most challenging to love people you run into are those who need love the most.

It's often because of that lack of love in their life that they strive to get attention, even if it has to be negative attention. If you don't feel like loving someone, you can still step out in faith and show love as a chosen course of action. Love is giving someone what they need the most when they deserve it the least, quite possibly at a high personal cost. We cannot force a feeling, but we can think and act lovingly, and then our feelings will follow—at least over time.

> *Love is giving someone what they need the most when they deserve it the least, quite possibly at a high personal cost.*

An interesting scientific fact is that the more we do things for others—basically loving on them, whether we feel the love or not, we will grow to love them over time. Interesting, isn't it? I think attitude has a lot to do with it. We need to do these things with a loving attitude, even if we don't feel it yet. Again, this is a choice.

When we step out of our comfort zone to do something like this, the other person may or may not change based on our change of behavior towards them, but it changes us—for the better. You will feel so much better about yourself. So you are a winner on some level when you do this.

The most important tip I can throw in here regarding "Love" is that we are commanded to do so in the Bible, first in the Old Testament—in Deuteronomy 6:5. Jesus repeats it as recorded in three of the gospels by summarizing all of the law and prophets in the most important commandment: We are to love the Lord our God with all our heart, soul, mind, and strength, and our neighbor as ourselves. If we do that, all the other fruit and commandments will fall into place. Who is our neighbor? Whoever is in front of us. It could be your spouse, an ex, a family member, a coworker; you name it. We can't truly love God when we are withholding love from others in our lives. The more we are "in love" with Jesus, the more capacity we will have to love anyone in our life.

I know a great example of this. A friend of ours had fallen out of live with his wife and asked a friend to pray for him—that his love for his wife would return because divorce was not an option for him. His friend told him he just needed to love Jesus more and his love would return. It didn't really make senses to him at the time, but he trusted this highly respected friend so he intentionally devoted much more time to prayer, Bible study and worship and found himself falling in love with Jesus in a whole new way. Before he knew it, his love for his wife returned. They now have a marriage that is the envy of many who know them. As my former pastor used to say, "Not a sermon, just a thought."

Live honorably, love completely, and choose wisely—be Jesus with skin on. Choose to love someone today—no matter how unlovely they may seem. God bless, and I'll see you tomorrow!

DAY 3

John 15:1

Choose Joy

Joy might be a little more difficult for a non-Christian to understand because it is deeply rooted in faith. God teaches us absolute joy in the midst of sorrow as we turn to Him. It is not synonymous with happiness. Happiness is based on good fortune and depends on external circumstances—things going well and is also a choice. While happiness is nice, it is not enough to bring us lasting fulfillment, especially when circumstances change negatively.

On the other hand, Joy is an emotion of the Holy Spirit that arises from within us and is not affected by things that happen to us. It comes from within. It's an inside job and not dependent on circumstances or what we accomplish. It grows from remembering "whose" we are—the Lord's precious ones.

We can be heartbroken, and at the same time, be joyful. We can have things going on in our life that make us unhappy, but these things cannot rob us of the inner joy that we have in Christ. As a Christ-follower, our joy is based on our faith. It's not the joy that comes from earthly things. It is a joy whose unshakeable foundation is God. It is an indestructible joy that the Holy Spirit gives us. We *can* choose not to let circumstances rob us of our joy.

It's a sense of internal peace and contentment based on unchanging divine promises and eternal spiritual realities. It's the sense of well-being experienced by one who knows that all is well between oneself and the Lord. Joy is a gift from God, and as such, believers are not to manufacture it but to delight in the blessings they already possess.

Joy is not the absence of suffering. It is the presence of God. It's much like a muscle in that the more you choose to exercise it, the stronger it becomes. When we realize that all we do can have a God-serving focus, even mundane chores begin to feel less like drudgery and more like joy. Our busy lives are transformed by the privilege of serving Him by serving those around us.

I just learned an acrostic for **JOY** I'd like to share with you. It seems counter-cultural and certainly counter-intuitive, but as you may have already learned, it's in giving that we receive. Jesus first, Others second, Yourself last. When that is our mentality of priority, it builds joy into our lives.

Joy is not the absence of suffering. It is the presence of God.

I have known several individuals who have tragically lost a child or spouse. Of course, there was no happiness in their situations; however, these individuals expressed feeling a deep sense of joy in their souls during this time of grief and mourning. It was because of their faith in God and their knowledge that He is in control, His will is perfect, and He ensures us that He does not waste any experiences. They had experienced compassion, comfort, mercy, and grace that no one else would understand who has not been through a similar circumstance.

Trials don't bypass believers. But Jesus, who suffered and died for us, invites us to rest in Him so that even in the deepest valleys, we can rejoice! To quote Corrie ten Boom, the author of The Hiding Place, about her captivity in the German concentration camp during WWII, she said, "No matter how deep our darkness, He is deeper still."

God often provides joy and peace at times like these that are indescribable, indestructible, and unfathomable. John 15:11 tells us, "These things I have spoken to you, that my joy may be in you, and that your joy may be full."

Live honorably, love completely, and choose wisely—choose joy in the midst of whatever circumstances you find yourself. God bless, and I'll see you tomorrow!

Phil 4:6-7

DAY 4
Choose Peace

Are you experiencing some storms in your life right now? Do you lack peace in your life? It's important to know that even though you may feel like you are experiencing a situational tsunami in your life right now, if it were not for storms, there would be no rainbows. You can have incredible peace that passes all understanding.

Paul in Philippians 4:6-7 tells us, "Do not be anxious about anything, but in everything by prayer and supplication with thanksgiving let your requests be made known to God. And the peace of God, which surpasses all understanding, will guard your hearts and your minds in Christ Jesus."

Peace is another choice that we can make over fear and anxiety. It takes recognizing where our mind is going and living with the intention to make a U-turn and choosing peace.

Do you long for contentment—an internal peace? Do you struggle with fears that want to grip your heart? If you are a Christ-follower, you will know the Bible tells us in many places that we are to "Fear not." We know Christ is with us, in fact, He is in us in the person of the Holy Spirit to give us peace during difficult and uncertain times. Jesus provides the answer for our fear. I don't mean to minimize all that is going on. We cannot control many of the challenges and disappointments we face for sure, but we also do not have to be held captive to them. We *can* control how we respond to them.

19

We certainly live in a perilous time of adversity, tribulation, difficulty, and uncertainty. The promise Jesus gave the disciples holds true for us when He said in John 16:33: "I have said these things to you, that in Me you may have peace. In the world, you will have tribulation. But take heart; I have overcome the world," The command not to fear, or "fear not," is the most common commandment in the Bible. God created us to live in peace, not in fear.

As a Christ-follower, you understand perfect love casts out fear (1 John 4:18). Suppose you have experienced the saving grace and love of Jesus Christ. In that case, you know it is possible to experience peace when encountering the storms of life.

Peace comes in knowing that God's grace is sufficient and will sustain us even in our most difficult situations.

Peace comes from salvation—deliverance from our enemy—in our case, our sin. Romans 5:1 tells us, "Therefore since we have been justified by faith, we have peace with God through our Lord Jesus Christ." You notice that is present tense, "have" peace with God. This isn't just for when we die. It is for now and forever.

Contentment is not something to achieve; it is a secret to be discovered. We can learn so much from Paul. We need to understand that internal peace is not dependent on our circumstances. Peace comes in knowing that God's grace is sufficient and will sustain us even in our most difficult situations. It's not the absence of pressure, but the presence of God and our attitude toward His provision, during our stress.

The fact you have a relationship with God places immeasurable value on your life. The treasure of God's wisdom and knowledge is available to you through Christ as well as His perfect love. You now have access to the peace that passes all understanding and compassion for others that is supernatural. When Jesus lives in you, everything available to Him also dwells in you.

Today's call to action: When adversity hits, remember to call on the peace of God that is available to you by the Holy Spirit that lives inside you. Choose not fear or anxiety, but peace.

Live honorably, love completely, and choose wisely— choose peace today. God bless, and I'll see you tomorrow.

When anxiety hits - seek God's presence. TRUST

DAY 5

Proverbs 15:1

Choose Patience

Patience is defined as: "the state of endurance under difficult circumstances, which can mean persevering in the face of delay or provocation without negatively acting on annoyance or anger. It's exhibiting mercy when under strain. Patience also refers to the character trait of being steadfast." It's also translated as "longsuffering," the opposite of "quick anger," resentment, or revenge, and thus epitomizes Jesus Christ. It endures injustice and troublesome circumstances with hope for coming relief.

Patience is a choice and refers to the sum total of our habits. We can't claim to be a kind person unless we are habitually kind, showing kindness without even thinking about it. Patience is developed during circumstances where we are forced to choose restraint when tempted to get angry or impatient. One of the marks of an authentic Christian is their ability to exhibit abiding patience and boundless endurance during trying times. It's an outgrowth of humility and gentleness and shows maturity of character. We will be discussing these in other devotions.

Impatience has to be one of the greatest struggles we face, and it just seems to accelerate with time. We live in a "microwave" generation where we expect instant results. Patience is a fundamental character trait that does not come naturally to most people.

It is a fundamental building block of wholeness in our lives. It all starts with our attitude, and we will find that being patient in one area of our lives will help us become patient in other areas. It's a process.

You know the saying, "You get a lot more with sugar than with vinegar?" That is so true. Harsh words will only reap the same. It's a calm, quiet, patient response that fosters an atmosphere of understanding and improves friendships, marriages, and work relationships.

Patience is an outgrowth of humility and gentleness and shows maturity of character.

Just like it's easier to love someone who loves us rather than loving someone who has been unloving towards us, the same is true in that it's much easier to be patient with people who are patient with us. But if we withdraw from an impatient person, or give a sharp retort in response to their inappropriate behavior, we lose the opportunity to see the power that patience can have. Proverbs 15:1 can come in handy here, "A soft answer turns away wrath, but a harsh word stirs up anger."

None of us is perfect. All of us have experienced some situations where someone has created tension by being impatient and failing to control their tongue. When this happens, we experience feelings of hurt, anger, disappointment, and frustration. At this point, what matters is how we respond to that person.

Are we going to stoop to their level, lash out at them with harsh, bitter, condemning words, which will make the situation worse? Or are we going to pause and try to understand that person's thoughts and feelings that might have prompted their poor behavior? I love this quote from the book Peter Pan, written by J.M. Barrie, "Be kinder than necessary; for everyone you meet is fighting some kind of battle."

We may not like their behavior, but if we understand what's going on in their mind and heart, we can then give a more constructive response. Whenever faced with this type of situation, we choose either to retaliate, lash out with hurtful words, or we can listen, and seek to understand by asking questions, and then choose to speak with words that bring healing.

When we decide to be patient with someone and to hear them out rather than jump to conclusions and respond to confusing or inappropriate behavior in haste, we can gain a much deeper understanding of that person. Isn't it interesting that we are much more likely to speak healing words when we listen (especially with our heart) before speaking? This gives us an opportunity to affirm their value—while maintaining an attitude of patience, improving our chances of contentment, and successful and productive interactions that demonstrate authentic love.

As Gary Chapman shares in his book, Love as a Way of Life, "Patience gives us the freedom to let go of our need to be right all the time. It allows us the peace of putting relationships before the selfish desires that can rob us of joy. Like every trait of a loving person, patience begins with one choice followed by another until it becomes a beautiful habit."

On that note, live honorably, love completely, and choose wisely—choose patience today. God bless, and I'll see you to

DAY 6 *Phil 2:4*

Choose Kindness

As a matter of discipline and a demonstration of good manners, one can be kind in specific situations without being loving, but one cannot love without being kind. Being "kind" in the former sense is what we usually refer to as being "nice."

In a biblical sense, genuine kindness is a charitable behavior marked by a mild disposition, pleasantness, tenderness, and tender concern for others, treating them gently. God's goodness in action towards others permeates the entire person, mellowing all such aspects.

Kindness is love in action and is, therefore, a practical expression of love. When the Holy Spirit produces kindness in our lives, we become the hands, feet, and mouthpieces of God as we love those in need. We all have needs of some sort and need someone in our lives who is kind and can offer support when our burdens are too heavy to carry alone. Kind people are sensitive to the hurts and needs of others. Philippians 2:4 says, "Let each of you look not only to his own interests, but also to the interests of others."

As God's children, we are to reflect our Heavenly Father's kindness. We are to be kind because He is kind to us. Grace and kindness go hand in hand. We are to be gracious in treating family and friends and how we relate to our neighbors and coworkers daily. It means being part of what God is already doing in our world to bring hope to the sick and needy, the frightened, and the victims of injustice. It's being Jesus with skin on. It's being an extension of Him to whomever we come into contact.

We are to be an example of His character and an expression of His love. When the Holy Spirit produces God's kindness in us, we become humble servants who actively reflect His impartial love and compassion, being gracious in how we treat everyone in our sphere of influence. Our disposition towards others becomes like that of Jesus Christ—gentle, understanding, and supportive. Through us, He can extend His mercy and hope to a hurting world.

You give and receive kindness in some form or another every day, probably without even thinking about it. The critical point to attach to this is to think of ways to be kind to others, recognize when others have been kind to you, and respond with gratefulness. When this has not been a former habit, it can blow someone away to consciously give and receive such care.

Kindness is love in action and is therefore, a practical expression of love.

This attribute is contagious, and with a bit of practice, can become a way of life. Because it is contagious, there is a tendency for those who have been recipients of an act of kindness to pass it along to others, paying it forward. Acts of kindness improve the lives of the recipients and bring great satisfaction to the giver. It's the joy of putting someone else's need before our own. We are not to be looking for something in return. We're kind just because we care about them and want to serve them.

In relationships where we practice kindness, we talk to one another with respect. We speak up and talk through their issues using words that affirm one another rather than pointing an accusing finger. The more we practice kindness in our relationships, the more it will be reciprocated, and the more it will become a way of life.

Interestingly enough, the kinder we act towards others, the warmer we will feel towards them. It is a remarkable observation that small acts of kindness in daily life can have a massive impact on improving, restoring, or even saving relationships. Our kindness shows how much we value one another. Putting other's interests before our own is crucial to make relationships work.

An excellent book on kindness is Alan Luks' book, The Healing Power of Doing Good. He explains how scientific studies have shown that when performing an act of kindness, the brain releases endorphins producing a feeling of euphoria and peacefulness called a helper's high, much akin to the phenomenon which runners experience. It can improve the immune system, reverse feelings of depression, hostility, and isolation. It increases one's sense of self-worth, optimism, and overall life satisfaction. It reaffirms that when we care for others, we are caring for ourselves. It kind of makes you want to go out and do all sorts of good, doesn't it?

On that note, live honorably, love completely, and choose wisely— choose kindness today. God bless, and I'll see you tomorrow!

DAY 7
Choose Goodness

Kindness acts
goodness heart
attitude.
Ephesians 2:20

While kindness and goodness are not synonymous, they are two words that hold very similar meanings. We described kindness previously as acts of courtesy towards others. On the other hand, goodness refers more to the heart attitude—one that is morally upright and virtuous.

Kindness refers more to the actions of love that come from the heart of goodness—a heart striving to do good and promote good. It's the goodness inside of us that motivates us to do kind things towards one another. It comes from a place of selflessness in which we place the needs of others before our own. So the two terms go hand-in-hand.

Goodness is not about doing elaborate things to gain recognition. Often, it's the small acts of goodness we do throughout our day that mean the most to those around us.

Any goodness we possess is a gift from God, as it certainly does not come naturally. It is He who gives us the desire and power to do good. When we become Christians, we are created with goodness in mind as we are given a new nature with a desire to do good. Ephesians 2:20 tells us "For we are His workmanship, created in Christ Jesus for good works, which God prepared beforehand, that we should walk in them." We must guard our heart and mind against planting thoughts and even images in our subconscious mind from where they could erupt to interfere with our desire to do the right thing.

We must develop convictions to stand up for what we know to be right, hate what is evil, and cling to what is good as we are encouraged to do in Romans 12:9. We are to have the courage to be different—not just avoiding evil, but being enthusiastic about doing good.

The goodness inside motivates us to do right and honorable things and speak in ways that are edifying to others. However, goodness can also drive us to righteous indignation. If we have a heart of inner goodness, it motivates us to be noble in our life. We are called to be "Salt and Light"—indicating zealous activity in doing good.

It is active, maybe even to the point of being aggressive. Goodness is not always carried out with kindness if "tough love" is necessary to carry out what is right and just. Therefore, goodness may come across as a harsher element in the exemplary character. Sometimes we may experience righteous outrage.

> It's the small acts of goodness we do throughout our day that mean the most to those around us.

Remember when Jesus, in righteous anger, cleared the temple of the money changers and merchants who had turned a place of worship into a marketplace? He was still good but firm and came across as harsh as He made clear their sin and need for repentance.

We are called to be men and women of goodness in our world. We need to be living the kind of goodness that can be kind but firm. Simultaneously, it is more than the excellence of character; it is character energized, expressing itself in active good. God can, and often does correct, sometimes very severely, as He exercises His goodness. Occasionally, we are called to do the same as an act of goodness.

The life of Jesus Christ is the perfect example of goodness, as He died on the cross for humanity's sins to give us the gift of eternal life. His ministry and sacrifice is an example of God's goodness toward humankind.

We are called as Christians to live in a way that reflects the character of Christ. Matthew 5:16 says, "In the same way, let your light shine before others, so that they may see your good works and give glory to your Father who is in heaven."

Live honorably, love completely, and choose wisely—choose goodness today. God bless, and I'll see you tomorrow!

DAY 8
Choose Faithfulness

Our best living example and faithfulness model is Jesus and how He perfectly completed every assignment the Father gave Him. Throughout His life, He consistently sought to be in tune with the Father.

He is so faithful to love us unconditionally even while we don't deserve it—which, by the way, is all the time. Someone faithful is reliable. This describes a person who is trustworthy and will always stand up for God's way. We can count on and should work at imitating God's faithfulness.

When we are faithful to Him, we walk with Him no matter what might happen to us because we can rely on His faithfulness to us. Throughout the Bible, we are urged to be bold in our faith to discover the benefits of God's love and faithfulness. When we are faithful to honor God, He will honor us.

We demonstrate our faithfulness when we put our faith into action, keeping our commitments and promises, being trustworthy, and living a consistent life with our words, beliefs, and Scriptures.

Another word for faithful is "steadfast." It means to be continually dedicated, dependable, stable, and unswerving. To be faithful means to be loyal, devoted, trustworthy, and unwavering. We demonstrate these traits by how we speak about others when they are not present. The most revealing way we can show our character is how we describe another's.

35

I'm reminded of the Marine Corps motto instituted back in 1883. Latin for always faithful, *Semper Fidélis* exhorts and guides Marines to remain faithful to the mission at hand, to each other, to the Corps, and country no matter what. Becoming a Marine is a transformation that cannot be undone, and *Semper Fi* reminds them of that. A marine is challenged to forever live by the ethics and values of the Corps.

Here are some pointers for those of us who are married: Just as faithfulness is a pillar in the Christ-follower's life, it also needs to be a pillar in the life of a married person. It is faithfulness that holds up and sustains the life of a marital relationship. It is the thread of hope for reconciliation when a relationship suffers. Because faithfulness is essential to our relationships, it is the one area of our life where we hurt the most when it is no longer there.

BIG TRUTH

The goal of faithfulness is not that we will do work for God but that He will be free to do His work through us.

We must be faithful in our allegiance to our Creator. Like many other things in life, faithfulness is a choice. No one can make anyone else faithful or unfaithful. It is a personal choice that begins in our hearts and minds and manifests itself in our actions. It is characterized by our unwavering trust in God and our trustworthiness.

The sooner we decide to be faithful to God, the sooner we will address any negative issues that might arise and the healthier our relationships will be. As a Christ-follower, it is essential to be faithful to God. It's one thing to believe in Him, but quite another to be faithful to Him. When we are truly faithful to God, it shapes the way we live. For example, we commit to be loyal in our relationships and to love others truly. It requires us to submit our ways to God.

Being faithful to Jesus Christ is one of the hardest things we try to do. For some reason, we find it easier to be faithful to do our work, serve others, or anything else. Still, we tend to treat God as if He were a genie designed only to bless us, and Jesus as just one of His workers.

The goal of faithfulness is not that we will do work for God but that He will be free to do His work through us. God calls us to His service and places tremendous responsibility on us. While He is full of grace, mercy and forgiveness when we fail, He expects our compliance without complaint or an explanation from Him. That is called surrender and obedience which we will discuss in greater detail in a later devotion. He wants to be able to use us for His glory like He used His own Son.

Just as breathing is an ongoing, lifelong exercise, so is the choice to remain faithful—not just in big things—but also in the small things that might seem insignificant—whatever we are called to do. The expiration date of our faithfulness to God is our death. Likewise, according to marriage vows, we are to be faithful until we are parted by death.

Food for thought: Is there anything holding you back from being sold out in your faithfulness to God and others? Your faithfulness can have an enormous impact on others. How are you demonstrating your faithfulness that is visible to outsiders?

Live honorably, love completely, and choose wisely—choose faithfulness today. God bless, and I'll see you tomorrow!

DAY 9 Matthew 11:29

Choose Gentleness

In Greek, (*praotes*) is the most untranslatable of words. In the New Testament, it has three primary meanings.

1. It means being submissive to the will of God.
2. It means being teachable, not too proud to learn.
3. But most of all, it means being considerate.

Aristotle defined *praotes* as the mean between excess of anger and excessive angerlessness, the quality of the man who was always angry at the right time and never at the wrong time. What throws most light on its meaning is that its adjective form, *praus* is used to describe an animal, like a wild stallion, which has been contained and brought under control. So the word speaks of that self-control which Christ alone can give.

Gentleness is not a personality type. You cannot get a pass by saying, "I'm just not a gentle person." A working definition might be something like "deciding only to use the least amount of force necessary to accomplish what's right." A tamed horse is just as strong as a wild horse, but its strength is under control, bottled up for the master's use.

Biblical humility and gentleness have trusting and yielding one's spirit towards God at their core. One would think that gentleness would imply weakness, but it's the opposite. It is not being a doormat as some might suggest but is strength under control. For example, when Jesus was being mocked and flogged, He demonstrated His gentleness towards His accusers when He could've had a legion of angels swoop down to save Him. Yet He chose to respond with gentleness and humility, accepting God's plan for His life. It's the weak who are arrogant, prideful, pushy, rude, mean spirited, and engage in gossip.

Although gentleness is an aspect of being kind, this choice does not adequately describe the qualities the original word implies. A person exhibiting gentleness is considerate and courteous in conduct and correction. They are mild-spirited. Those who God transforms are humbled before God, and the meekness of their heart is a delight to Him. Jesus taught gentleness as a virtue.

When we live a life of gentleness, we honor Him. In the Sermon on the Mount—in Matthew 5:5, "Jesus said, "Blessed are the meek, for they shall inherit the earth." This means that the meek will experience abundant blessings while here on this earth. As they delight themselves in the Lord, He will give them the desires of their hearts as found in Psalm 37:4. "Gentleness," often translated as "meekness," is the willingness to suffer injury or insult rather than to inflict such hurts. We don't hear much about gentleness in our world because we don't understand what it really means to be gentle.

> *Those who God transforms are humbled before God, and the meekness of their heart is a delight to Him.*

Gentle people extend grace to others. They are willing to yield to others rather than always demand their way. They are not quarrelsome, hear others out, and are eager to serve and submit to others in the bond of peace. Gentle people take the time to figure out the most appropriate response, rather than being driven by their first emotional response. They are careful with others' weaknesses and wounds and use it as a barometer to respond.

They choose to respond to injustice without vengeance or bitterness. Gentle people genuinely know how to speak the truth in love. They know how to respond in a godly way to difficult people.

Gentle people don't overreact, driven by their own emotions, but understand Romans 12:17-18, where Paul tells us we are not to repay evil for evil but to do what is honorable. As far as it depends on us, we are to live peaceably with everyone. Jesus modeled that for us, and He empowers us to do the same.

You will notice that a lot of these character qualities are similar to an extent. This one overlaps with humility as defined, along with meekness as an inner grace. Gentleness requires humility and the two are often linked in the New Testament like when Jesus said in Matthew 11:29, "Take my yolk upon you and learn from me, for I am gentle and lowly in heart, and you will find rest for your souls."

If you struggle with a gentle spirit, ask Jesus to help you be more like Him. That is the goal anyway, isn't it, to be more like Christ? He will help you.

Live honorably, love completely, and choose wisely—choose gentleness today. God bless, and I'll see you tomorrow.

DAY 10
Choose Self-Control

When Paul wrote Galatians, listing the fruit of the Spirit, it would seem that God had him save this virtue for last because, besides love, with which he starts the list, it is the most important and foundational to all the rest. We need self-control to have biblical love, joy, peace, patience, kindness, goodness, faithfulness, and gentleness. What we see here is "love" and "self-control" as bookends of the fruit of the Spirit. As the Spirit works in and on us to get us to develop these attributes in our lives, they require us to cultivate self-control—the positive use rather than the abuse of our God-given abilities and freedoms.

Just as a side note, have you noticed that the "Fruit of the Spirit" is singular and not plural? It's not referred to as the "fruits" of the Spirit. We are not to pick and choose the fruit we like and disregard what we don't. They come as a package, and over time, as we mature in our faith and deepen our commitment and walk with the Lord, they should become present and active in our lives.

The word "self-control" comes from the Greek word for strength, which relates self-control to the strength it takes to control our will, emotions, mind, and body. Vines Expository Dictionary defines self-control as "the ability and power not to abuse the powers God has given us." Some examples of this would be everything from our eating habits, vocabulary, sex, body, possessions, relationships, a bent toward anger, or political power over those weaker than we are.

Self-control, among other things, is discipline, which gives us victory over the wrong pulls of our mind and body. It's the ability to exercise restraint or control over one's feelings, emotions, reactions, etc. Self-control is a virtue that makes one able to master themselves so that they are fit to be the servant of others.

Our family relationships are so intimate that it gives us plenty of opportunities to practice and exercise self-control daily. Through the Holy Spirit, we are given the fruit of self-control, and that which we cannot do by our own power is done for us. Paul reminds us in Galatians 2:20, "I have been crucified with Christ. It is no longer I who live, but Christ who lives in me. And the life I now live in the flesh I live by faith in the Son of God, who loved me and gave himself for me."

> *Displaying self-control is often a matter of responding rather than reacting.*

Self-control helps us to resist temptation and avoid conforming to the things of this world. It guides our decisions, and it correlates with how we show the other fruit in our lives.

For example, patience (like all the other fruit) requires self-control. Proverbs 14:29 says, "Whoever is slow to anger (*in other words, is patient*) has great understanding, but he who has a hasty temper exalts folly." Our sinful nature leads us to give in to our temper, but we are called to rise above this and show patience. When we do that, we are exhibiting self-control.

Displaying self-control is often a matter of responding rather than reacting. When we react to a situation, we let our emotions take control. We are more likely to become defensive and say hurtful things.

Responding, however, involves developing a thoughtful response that is guided by reason more than emotions.

We are reminded in 1 Corinthians 10:13 that, "No temptation has overtaken you that is not common to man. God is faithful, and He will not let you be tempted beyond your ability, but with the temptation He will also provide the way of escape, that you may be able to endure it."

We need to realize that there is not temptation unless, first, there was a desire for something. Sometimes we need self-control to temper our desires, so they do not become temptations.

As always, we can look to Jesus as our example of self-control as He gave us the perfect example of how to live out all this fruit in our lives. While it may seem challenging to demonstrate self-control, the rewards will be great, and it is imperative if we are to have a positive, impactful influence on our corner of the world.

Live honorably, love completely, and choose wisely—choose self-control today. God bless, and I'll see you tomorrow!

DAY 11
Choose Humility

I heard a definition I love and always remembered: "Humility is not thinking less of yourself, but thinking of yourself less." To take that even further, "Humility is not thinking of yourself at all." It is the most foundational Christian virtue and is the first Beatitude mentioned in the "Sermon on the Mount." It is the opposite of self-sufficiency and speaks of recognizing one's utter spiritual bankruptcy apart from God.

Humility is the perfect antidote to the "self-love" that poisons human relationships. It certainly does not come naturally. We have to work at it intentionally. Years ago, I realized how far I fell short in this area, so when I got dressed in the morning, I started praying that the Lord would "clothe" me with the humility of Christ. Putting on clothes is a daily activity, so being clothed with the humility of Christ needs to be a planned daily activity.

Maybe we should look at the antonym for humility as well to define what humility is not. The opposite of humility is arrogance or pride. We must keep in mind the Scripture from James 4:6, which states, "God opposes the proud, but gives grace to the humble" We cannot be both, so we have to choose.

Humility causes us to be more focused on our sin rather than that of others we are in a relationship with who might be causing us pain. If we're humble, we won't judge or shift blame to others, requiring them to acknowledge their sins before recognizing our own. It gives others the benefit of the doubt. It plays a massive role in a loving relationship when we intentionally and voluntarily become subservient to the other person.

Many people think of humility as a weak character trait—something they would only be willing to show if they didn't mind being walked on by other people. However, when Jim Collins was researching for his book, *From Good to Great*, he discovered a surprising characteristic among the most successful CEOs he interviewed. They were some of the most humble people he'd ever met. Each of them was quick to praise their team and their employees for their companies' success and did not take the credit themselves. They seemed reasonably at peace, affirming the value of others over themselves. Authentic humility affirms the work of others and shows strength better than weakness.

The desire to be first in our culture is so ingrained in us that some question if we can learn humility. When we look at the behavior of young children, it's obvious it must be learned. That is *not* something we are born with. Humility is developed and evidenced when we choose to put others first, even if it means making a sacrifice.

> *Humility is developed and evidenced when we choose to put others first, even if it means making a sacrifice.*

The greatest example of humility I can think of in the form of being a servant (besides Christ humbling Himself to His death on the cross to save us from our sins) is His example in the Upper Room when He donned a towel, picked up a pitcher of water and a basin and knelt to wash each of the disciples' feet. This is a job usually reserved for the lowliest of servants. There was no servant present to perform that task as they gathered there in that room on the night of the Passover, and none of the disciples offered to stoop to that position, so

Jesus did it Himself. He even washed Judas's feet knowing he was about to betray Him.

One by one, He washed their feet as an example of humility and servanthood. He wanted them to learn from this to serve one another. As they would look back on this night, later on, they would then see it also as an example of what was to come as He humbly gave up His life for them.

In John 13: 14-17, this is recorded: "If I then, your Lord and Teacher, have washed your feet, you also ought to wash one another's feet. For I have given you an example, that you also should do just as I have done to you. Truly, truly, I say to you, a servant is not greater than his master, nor is a messenger greater than the one who sent Him. If you know these things, blessed are you if you do them."

Humility is recognizing that you are no better or worse than anyone else. You are just as strong or weak as the next person. It's okay to accept and appreciate affirmation as long as we're not prideful about it. We should just long to be all God created us to be. If we get accolades for that, we need to be sure not to be prideful but to accept the recognition with humility and, when possible, to give glory to God.

What some might call a "false" humility, Gary Chapman talks about "pride in reverse," saying that, "Pride is not the only enemy to humility. Failing to recognize our worth also keeps us from loving others. If we are truly humble, we will not put ourselves down. Just as love causes us to recognize the value of others, it also calls us to affirm our value." We need to give thanks for who we are and recognize our value and self-worth.

In the end, God is much more interested in whether we are humble than whether or not we're right. He's more interested in who we become inwardly than what we accomplish outwardly.

Live honorably, love completely, and choose wisely—choose to be humble today. God bless, and I'll see you tomorrow!

DAY 12
Choose Forgiveness

This is a hard but very important topic and I hate to start this devotional out on a negative note. Still, I must say that if we have difficulty forgiving someone, we need to remember what Christ did for us on the cross. If He can forgive us for all our sins (past, present, and future), which He has, we can certainly forgive someone who has wronged us.

Think about that. Suppose you are a Christ-follower and have accepted the death of Jesus on your behalf, saving you from endless destruction forever and giving you eternal life in heaven—forgiving all your sins. In that case, you *must* pay it forward to those who have sinned against you. It doesn't matter how much someone may have hurt you.

Besides God being "love," His nature is forgiveness. As Christ-followers, we *must* follow His example. If we insist on withholding forgiveness from anyone, our worship and prayers are futile. We must follow David's example in Psalm 139 and ask God to search our heart and reveal areas where we are harboring resentment and areas where we need to ask and/or receive forgiveness. We need to ask God to make us like Christ, so even during persecution, we can imitate Him and say, "Father, forgive them."

In Scripture, Jesus told us we can expect forgiveness from God as we forgive those who sin against us. He will forgive us in the same way we forgive others (Matthew 6:15). This declaration does not suggest God will take away the salvation/justification from those who have already received the free pardon, which He extends to all believers. Forgiveness, in that sense—a permanent and complete acquittal from the guilt and ultimate penalty of sin—belongs to all who are in Christ. However, Scripture also teaches God disciplines His children who disobey Him; and a lack of forgiveness on our part is a sin that will rob us of intimacy with Him.

Jesus never said certain offenses are unworthy of our forgiveness. We have no biblical excuse for allowing any unforgiveness in our hearts. No offense committed against us is so heinous that God's love cannot enable us to forgive. Forgiveness is not in any way a spiritual gift, a skill, or an inherited ability. It's not a personality; it's a choice—an act of the will, rather than a feeling. If we waited until we felt like forgiving anyone, we never would.

It's releasing another from the penalty of sin against us, so hopefully, you can restore the relationship. Depending on the other party, the restoration of the relationship is not always possible, but it should be our goal. It's canceling a debt owed to you and giving up any right for retribution. I know you may not feel like it, and think a particular individual doesn't deserve to be forgiven, particularly if they have not even asked for it. That's okay. We certainly didn't deserve God's forgiveness, yet He forgave us anyway.

Forgiveness cannot change your past, but it can change your future.

Forgiveness has little advantage to the one who caused pain. It mainly benefits you, the one who has been hurt. In reality, it is a gift you give to yourself. Otherwise, the bitterness of unforgiveness will eat away and probably even spill over into your other relationships. A spirit of unforgiveness is toxic.

Not forgiving someone is like drinking poison, hoping that that the other person will die. Jesus commands us to forgive as an act of obedience. When we do, the feelings will follow—maybe not right away, but they will eventually if you have genuinely forgiven and turned the results over to God.

Forgiveness is not just a "one-time" event but an ongoing process of mentally letting it go. If a person deserves God's wrath, that's God's business. Let Him deal with this person in His way. When someone offends us, our responsibility is to respond with forgiveness (Matthew 5:44). The real test of complete forgiveness is the ability to pray for God's blessing of the person we have forgiven—the person who wronged us.

You can be sure God will take the responsibility to see that justice is done. He loves people too much to allow sin to go unchecked. God is "just," which is all part of being "love." He alone can be sure justice is carried out appropriately.

I love this quote by Pastor Andy Stanley: "The one who benefits the most from forgiveness is the one who grants it, not the one who receives it." We cannot have an intimate relationship with the Father or experience a victorious Christian life when we hold a grudge against our brother, spouse, neighbor, or whomever. This is a difficult challenge today for many people, but crucial to ensure your intimacy with Jesus, which has to be our heart's desire. Forgiveness cannot change your past, but it can change your future. It will produce freedom that is not possible when harboring resentment.

Who do you need to forgive or ask for forgiveness today? Don't hang onto that resentment for one more day!

Live honorably, love completely, and choose wisely—choose to forgive someone today. God bless, and I'll see you tomorrow!

DAY 13
Choose Grace

What is grace exactly? As a Christ-follower, we look at grace as God's kindness and favor to all of us who certainly don't deserve it. Someone created an acronym to define it as **G**od's **R**iches at **C**hrist's **E**xpense. What we deserve is eternal separation from a holy God because of our sinful nature. But for those of us who have embraced and accepted Jesus's sacrificial death on the cross in our place, taking the penalty of our sin on Himself, we acknowledge that we have been saved by grace, through faith and that we did nothing on our own to merit salvation.

Ephesians 2:8-9 tell us, "For by grace you have been saved through faith. And this is not your own doing; it is the gift of God, not a result of works, so that no one may boast." Grace is so much a part of God and so inextinguishable that He can no more hide it than the sun can hide its brightness. Just like God is love, God is grace. It's part of who He is. It is His grace that transforms us and gives us the power to change.

So what do we do with that grace? If we are committed to the challenge of living our life in a way that we are an extension of Christ with the goal to become like Him, then we pay that grace forward. It's like forgiveness in that we have been given so much undeserved grace and favor that we have no excuse not to pay it forward to those we encounter. This is not something we can do in our own strength, but remember you have the Holy Spirit inside you to give you the strength, courage, and power to do anything in line with His will.

Our God is lavish in His grace. He often freely and liberally dispenses His goodness without even the slightest bit of cooperation and contribution on our part. Still, we must be careful not to let sin stifle or become obstacles to that marvelous grace. Sin will block our intimacy with God. In my book, *Living the Life You Always Wanted*, I have a chapter that speaks to the obstacles to grace we need to recognize and avoid. The condition for experiencing the *fullness* of God's grace and blessings is absolute surrender to Him.

One thing I think that is so awesome about God's grace is that He always shows up with just the amount of grace we need at just the right time—in the moment that we need it. He doesn't give it as a reserve ahead of time, and He is never late. He is always right on time with exactly the amount we need to cover whatever we are going through. And, we can count on it to be sufficient, like the manna God provided for the Israelites in the wilderness. He provided just the amount they needed each day.

> *We have been given so much undeserved grace and favor that we have no excuse not to pay it forward.*

Remember when Paul had his thorn in the flesh, whatever that was, and he asked God to take it away in 2 Corinthians 12:9? God told him "My grace is sufficient for you, for my power is made perfect in weakness." then Paul stated, "Therefore I will boast all the more gladly of my weaknesses, so the power of Christ may rest upon me."

There is no pain so deeply embedded in your heart that God's grace cannot reach down and at least provide comfort, if not eradicate it over time, and bring healing. Throughout the Bible, we see examples of the grace of God, and Jesus unquestionably modeled it to the fullest as He offered His life of righteousness in exchange for our sins when He took the punishment we deserved and died on the cross in our place.

What are you going to do with the grace you have been so graciously given? To whom do you need to extend grace today?

Live honorably, love completely, and choose wisely—choose to be gracious today. God bless, and I'll see you tomorrow!

DAY 14
Choose Mercy

While grace is defined as getting what we don't deserve (unmerited favor), mercy is defined as *not* getting what we *do* deserve—the wrath and condemnation of God. These two words mean different things but go hand in hand. God freely gives both to those who will humble themselves before Him and accept responsibility for their sins. Mercy is perhaps one of the most defining qualities of God, and without it, none of us would be here.

Miraculously, God in His mercy does not give us the penalty that our sins deserve. He is unchangeably compassionate and kind. He forgives and restores those who humbly repent and turn to Him in believing faith. His mercies are new every morning as declared in one of my favorite verses, Lamentations, 3:22-23 "The steadfast love of the Lord never ceases; His mercies never come to an end; they are new every morning; great is your faithfulness." I have a friend who often says, "Thank heavens, it's a 'Do over' day!" Everything God does in us and through us is because of His mercy.

Another great verse that speaks to this is Ephesians 2: 4-5: "But God, being rich in mercy, because of the great love with which He loved us, even when we were dead in our trespasses, made us alive together with Christ—by grace, you have been saved." Another well-known verse that speaks to God's mercy is Psalm 103:8, "The Lord is merciful and gracious, slow to anger and abounding in steadfast love." We can count on Him to show forgiveness to all those who turn from their sins and follow Christ.

God's mercy is not a matter of forgetting or ignoring our sin; rather, His mercy is seen in His choice not to hold our sins against us if we repent and believe. If we painstakingly denounce our sins, God will thoroughly forgive them. We must understand and acknowledge our depravity and the depth of our sin before we can fully repent and appreciate what a great gift God's mercy is toward us.

I find it interesting that the prophet Micah in 6:8 says we are to "love mercy." He doesn't just say to demonstrate or practice mercy, but to fall in love with it. That means to become its biggest fan. Having received mercy, we are to walk in assurance and thankfulness, using our gift of mercy as the lens through which we are to view anyone else's sin including that of our spouse, family members, others in our life. We are to extend mercy to them as well and as freely as it has been extended to us.

Mercy is wonderful. Without it, we would all be damned for eternity. Through His mercy, God made a way for us to enjoy eternal happiness instead of never-ending pain and torture. Mercy also allows us to have a positive impact on others. As fallen individuals who sin daily, we could never even begin to reach out to others to share the love of Christ unless every day we live in the joy of knowing that Jesus Christ's sacrifice on our behalf has set us free and washed us clean. If we love mercy, it means we love everything about it. Those who love mercy feel eager to show it to others. Mercy isn't an obligation grudgingly given in to—it's the love of one's life! It's their favorite practice.

> *We are to extend mercy to others as freely as it has been extended to us.*

60

One cannot sustain a close relationship without mercy. Our sin and guilt are so powerful that without mercy, every human connection will fail. James 2:13 says, "For judgment is without mercy to one who has shown no mercy. Mercy triumphs over judgment."

Your call to action today—meditate on mercy. Fall in love with it. Seek to understand what a gift God's mercy is that you have received. And then, from that foundation, explore the riches of extending this same mercy to others. We must pay it forward. If you're married, begin with your spouse, then other family members, then others in your sphere of influence.

Live honorably, love completely, and choose wisely—choose to be merciful today. God bless, and I'll see you tomorrow!

DAY 15
Choose Faith

First, let's define faith. Hebrews 11:1 is the famous passage that describes it for us as "the assurance of things hoped for and the conviction of things not seen." The word assurance here is the same Greek word for "exact representation." The "faith" described here involves the most solid possible conviction, the God-given present assurance of a future reality.

True faith is not based on empirical evidence, but divine assurance and is a gift of God. The word "faith" is mentioned from 175 times in the ESV to 254 times in the NIV Bible, but I will just mention a few verses about faith here.

Remember Ephesians 2:8 Paul tells us that we are saved by grace, through faith. Justification is entirely the work of Christ, and faith in Him secures this salvation and incentivizes us to become more Christ-like in the ongoing process of sanctification.

In Galatians 2:20, Paul says of himself after his conversion: "I have been crucified with Christ. It is no longer I who live, but Christ who lives in me. And the life I now live in the flesh I live by faith in the Son of God, who loved me and gave Himself for me." This is true for any of us who have given our hearts to Jesus.

In the first chapter of 1 Peter, the author is talking about our inheritance we receive as Christ-followers, but also about trials we are sure to have and he says, in verse 7, "So that the tested genuineness of your faith—more precious than gold that perishes though it is tested by fire—may be found to result in praise and glory and honor at the revelation of Jesus Christ. Though you have not seen Him, you love Him. Though you do not now see Him, you believe in Him and rejoice with joy that is inexpressible and filled with glory, obtaining the outcome of your faith, the salvation of your souls."

In 2 Corinthians 5:7, it says, "For we walk by faith, not by sight."

God is all about faith. Genuine faith will always produce authentic, faithful obedience. Faith in no way eliminates our problems, but helps us trust God in the midst of them. Nothing pleases God more than when we exercise faith—trusting and believing in Him. The only time Jesus rebuked His disciples was for their unbelief.

Remember when, during a storm on the Sea of Galilee, Jesus was walking on the water and He bid Peter to join Him upon his request? As long as Peter kept his eyes on Jesus, his faith was strong, and he was walking on water, but when he took his eye off Him and looked down into the raging waves, his faith failed him, and he started to drown until Jesus reached down to save him.

> Genuine faith will always produce authentic, faithful obedience.

An accurate measure of a person's faith is not just the first step of their faith journey but the subsequent steps after that. We must realize that if Jesus has called us to make the first step, He will provide a path for each step toward Him after that. Remember the story in Joshua 3 where God parted the Jordan River for the Israelites to cross? He didn't do it until they had first stepped into the water. They had to step out in faith before God stepped in and parted the waters for them.

The victorious Christian life is lived by faith, in a moment-by-moment surrender and obedience to God. It is a life rooted and grounded in faith and submission.

Fear shows a lack of faith and trust in God. A lack of faith or a spirit of unbelief is a byproduct of not knowing God. We need the courage to step out in faith to accomplish what God calls us to do. Whether or not we have faith in something will not determine or alter the truth about it. It is what it is, and we cannot debate it.

James 1:2-3 tells us that faith in our faithful God allows us to live fearlessly and show how He equips us to live no matter what we might face during uncertain times. Romans 4:21 tells us that knowing God gives us the complete assurance that He will fulfill His promises.

There is so much we could say here, but I promised to keep these devotionals short. How are you doing on your faith journey? How is God calling you to a stronger faith? What do you do in those difficult days when your faith falters, and visible challenges get the best of you? God, Himself will stoke the fire of our faith with His strength and power, and it's possible to experience Him as the unshakable foundation of faith. Sometimes He lets us experience adversity so we can discover He offers more than this fallen world can offer.

Live honorably, love completely, and choose wisely—choose faith today. God bless, and I'll see you tomorrow!

DAY 16
Choose Compassion

If you want to know the measure of your love for God, observe your love for your fellow man. Our compassion for others is an accurate gauge of our devotion to God. Practically speaking, we have compassion when we set aside indifference and connect with those in pain. This seems to be the first step toward healing.

A couple of verses that speak to that are from 1 John 4:7, 21: "Beloved, let us love one another, for love is from God, and whoever loves has been born of God and knows God.... And this commandment we have from Him: whoever loves God must also love his brother."

Our best model for compassion without question is Jesus Himself. To list a few examples: Remember when He saw the blind men in Matthew 20:34, "Jesus in pity touched their eyes, and immediately they recovered their sight." Then in Matthew 14:14 when He saw groups longing for His teaching, "He had compassion on them and healed their sick." Then in Mark 6:34, He noted the confusion of the people in the crowd following Him and "He had compassion on them because they were like sheep without a shepherd."

There are at least two things we can learn from Jesus in these examples:

First, He notices those around Him, so He was attuned to others and their needs. Suppose we are so absorbed in our feelings, problems, worries, or desires. In that case, we will not even notice the needs of others whom God has put in our path, missing or even ignoring the opportunity to help them.

Secondly, Jesus responds with compassion to people rather than reacting to them. There is a difference. Remember the story of the ten lepers that He healed in Luke 17:12-19 when they shouted at Him from a distance? Rather than being irritated by them, He listened to their request and met their need. Then there is the woman with the bleeding disorder in Matthew 9:20. Rather than chastising her for touching the hem of His garment, He took time to seek her out. He spoke to her, telling her that because of her faith, she was healed.

Our compassion for others is an accurate gauge of our devotion to God.

Here are three takeaways we can learn from these examples and three steps that can help us follow Christ's example and love with a tender heart.

1. **Build your empathy.** Spend some time putting yourself in someone else's shoes when you see their suffering or perhaps behaving poorly. This exercise can help you learn how to "Rejoice with those who rejoice and weep with those who weep (Romans 12:15).

2. **Learn to pause before speaking.** Scripture tells us in 1 Samuel 16:7, "Man looks on the outward appearance, but the LORD looks on the heart." To be compassionate toward others, we need to give the Holy Spirit time to override our tendency to judge. Without that, we may jump to conclusions about why someone might be behaving as they are.

3. **Recognize the barriers to compassion.** It's impossible to be annoyed and compassionate at the same time. Negative thoughts

such as various forms of aggravation are signs that we may be lacking compassion when dealing with others. Ephesians 4:31 tells us we need to "Let all bitterness and wrath and anger and clamor and slander be put away from you, along with all malice" that rules in our hearts. Ask God to help you "Be kind to one another, tenderhearted, forgiving one another, as God in Christ forgave you" (Ephesians 4:32).

Live honorably, love completely, and choose wisely—choose this day to cultivate a spirit of compassion. God bless, and I'll see you tomorrow!

DAY 17
Choose Hope

Do you, or have you, ever felt hopeless or that you were at the end of your rope and lost all hope? That is a dangerous and dark place to be. If you ever do feel that way, please talk to someone and get help. It's not uncommon for some people to find it very difficult to choose hope if their situation *seems* hopeless. Please remember that anything is possible with God.

What is hope? My former pastor used to say of Christ-followers, "our hope is not a 'hope so' hope, but a' know so' hope." I like that. It's "to look forward with confidence or expectation."

When we bring hope to someone struggling with this, we bring life. It is life-changing to finally believe in the hope that once was lost. It is more than just asking God for something we so badly need; we must expect our miracle. Somewhere while asking, believing, and expecting God to answer, we will find what we are looking for.

We live in such difficult times that there seem to be many hurts, problems, sicknesses, troubles, financial woes, family problems, world issues, political concerns, and so on. These issues can stack up so much that, understandably, many have lost hope. Sometimes we discover we put our hope in the wrong things.

Apart from God, it is easy to see our situation as hopeless. But with God's help, nothing is hopeless. He makes it possible to get through any situation, no matter how difficult it may be. It may not be tangible, but it is there for anyone willing to look to Jesus. He will meet you where you are to provide whatever you need to give you hope in your situation.

Suppose we had no Bible, no cross, no salvation, no empty tomb. Suppose we had nothing to hang on except, "Do your best, try to patch it up, do what you can." Oh, but we do have hope. There is a plan of redemption and a plan for the future.

God wants you to trust Him. It's essential to agree with God about your situation and turn it over to Him. What does God say about who you are and what His will is for your life? Rather than trust our feelings, we need to remember that God only has plans for us that are good. I am reminded of Jeremiah 29:11, where He says, "For I know the plans I have for you, declares the LORD, plans for welfare and not for evil, to give you a future and a hope."

With God's help, nothing is hopeless.

We do not need to be disappointed and feel alone. We can have hope! God's love will ignite the flames of hope we have buried deep inside our hearts. God's Word can encourage us as we read it with great anticipation and faith.

The Psalms are full of songs of hope, but Paul also reminds us of hope and gives encouragement in many of his letters. I am reminded of Romans 5:5, where he says, "And hope does not put us to shame, because God's love has been poured into our hearts through the Holy Spirit who has been given to us."

Here are a couple more really good verses also from Romans. Verse 12:12 says, " Rejoice in hope, be patient in tribulation, be constant in prayer." This one is especially good: Romans 15:13, "May the God of hope fill you with all joy and peace in believing, so that by the power of the Holy Spirit you may abound in hope."

I don't want this to be just another devotion. I want it to bring life to you. Like the Psalmists, try praying out loud the words of hope into your life and your situations. "I have hope! My hope is in the Lord! I will be strong and wait on the Lord. I trust God with my life and those I love." Speak these words every day. *Hope Is Real.* It comes from God! He has placed it in your heart. Speak it out and watch what God will do for you.

As you speak these words of God over yourself and your situation, your hope should come alive in your heart. What is your need today? Whatever it is, take it to Jesus. Is there someone in your life who needs an encouraging word? Speak words of hope that bring life. Hope is real and does not depend on our circumstances. We just need to try it. Remember Colossians 1:27, "Christ in you, the hope of glory." Jesus can and wants very much to be the "hope" for everyone. When storms come, and they will, we must learn to hold onto the hope that the world does not know—our "know so" hope.

Live honorably, love completely, and choose wisely—choose hope today. God bless, and I'll see you tomorrow!

DAY 18
Choose Holiness

What is holiness, and why is it important? Why choose to be holy? Is it even possible? One Bible dictionary defines holiness as "separation to God and conduct fitting for those separated." Holiness is not a human quality at all, like virtue. It's not something people do but something God does in us. He sets us apart for a purpose. This has to be one of the hardest attributes to grasp, at least for me, but I will do my best to describe it.

God is high and lifted up and set apart above His creation. He is absolute truth and His word defines absolute truth. He is always perfect with a purity that is incapable of being anything other than what it is. Holy is the way God is, and He is the standard. He has set us Christ-followers apart to be holy as He is holy. Because He is holy, all His attributes are holy. In the Bible, the word "holy" is used more than any other adjective to describe God's nature and character.

In Isaiah 6:3, the prophet describes seeing seraphim in the heavens singing, "Holy, holy, holy is the LORD of hosts; the whole earth is full of His glory!" One "holy" wasn't enough. He had to say it three times to emphasize it and then added, "The whole earth is full of His glory!"

Because holiness is the essence of God's character, it becomes our calling as His children by inheritance. In 1 Peter 1:14-16, the author says: "As obedient children, do not be conformed to the passions of your former ignorance, but as He who called you is holy, you also be holy in all your conduct, since it is written, 'You shall be holy, for I am holy.'"

Here's the best way to understand it: you are holy, and you have been called to be holy. If you are God's child, you stand before Him as righteous because the perfect righteousness of Jesus has been given over to your account. But there's a second aspect of this—In 1 Corinthians 6:19, 20, Paul tells us "Do you not know that your body is a temple of the Holy Spirit within you, whom you have from God? You are not your own, for you were bought with a price. So glorify God in your body."

To say you are holy means that you have been set apart by God's grace for God's purpose. When we are holy we are Christ-like. That is God's agenda for us, and our goal as a Christ-follower. Your allegiance is no longer to your success and happiness but the progress of His kingdom of glory and grace. Where and when do you do this? You do this wherever you are, whoever you're with, and in whatever you're doing.

> To say you are holy means that you have been set apart by God's grace for God's purpose

There's a third and final aspect: You have been called to holy living. This means that between the "already" of your conversion and the "not yet" of your home-going, obedience matters. Every thought, every desire, every word, every choice and every action must be done in a spirit of humble surrender to the commands of God.

Holiness is a quality of life that is winsome, loving, deeply caring, and morally pure. It is not an option for the Christ-follower. It not an external religious activity, but a condition of the heart and a purity of mind that expresses itself in a righteous lifestyle.

As you consider the impossibility of this call, take time to remember that God never calls you to a task without enabling you to do it. God calls us to be holy. Then, because there is no way we could ever do this on our own, He sends His Holy Spirit to live inside of us to have the wisdom and strength that we need to surrender to His holy call in all that we do. Wow, that's quite a calling and a lot to think about, isn't it?

As you ponder this, live honorably, love completely, and choose wisely—choose holiness today. God bless, and I'll see you tomorrow!

*Your allegiance is The Progress of His Kingdom of Glory r Grace.

Humble Surrender

DAY 19
Choose Truth, Honesty, and Integrity

Wikipedia defines honesty as *"a facet of moral character that denotes positive, virtuous attributes such as integrity, truthfulness, and straightforwardness along with the absence of lying, cheating, or theft."* This is a pretty good definition when you add "speaking the truth in love" with the emphasis on "in love."

I combined all three of these attributes since they are so similar and seem, at least to me, to be intertwined. We never outgrow our desire to be told the truth. Truth develops trust. Where there has been dishonesty, this leads to a lack of confidence. Once trust has been lost, it's challenging to regain. Dishonesty destroys relationships, whereas truth, combined with love, builds and restores relationships.

The critical element to keep in mind when telling the truth is to speak the truth in love. Loving words without telling the truth is dishonesty. Telling the truth without love is cruelty. When these two elements are part of our relationships (speaking the truth and speaking in love), we are on our way to developing a lifestyle and a habit of honesty. In Ephesians 4:16, Paul tells us that speaking the truth in love is directly tied to increased spiritual maturity.

Being authentic means living a life of honesty and integrity. Integrity means being true to yourself and living out who you are, not who you wish or hope to be. When living a life of integrity, we are free to acknowledge our weaknesses and vulnerability because we are secure in our relationship with Christ. Living a life of integrity points to honesty as a way of life. Such a lifestyle is one that others will desire to emulate. Just as the "integrity" of the building refers to it being structurally sound, so will *we* be considered structurally sound if we live a life reflecting truth showing integrity in all that we say and do. I can't claim to have integrity unless I live my life such that honesty is a habit. For example, a husband who is faithful to his wife *most* of the time is not faithful at all! Our behaviors define our character.

As hard as it may be, integrity calls us to take the risk of loving others by telling the truth when it's necessary, even if it hurts. Confronting someone with the truth, especially someone you love, can be challenging. Still, if love is behind both the struggle and the desire to engage, intending to get them back on the right track, the risk is well worth it.

Sometimes it's important to point out to someone we love that there needs to be a course correction in their life. Suppose we approach the conversation with the attitude of loving correction rather than criticism. In that case, possible acknowledgment of wrongdoing and the need to seek forgiveness are possible outcomes. That is an example of showing love honestly. Such conversations need to be bathed in prayer, initiated at an appropriate time, showered with love, showing an attitude of respect with the hope of a result being that of restoration of the individual.

> *Living a life of integrity points to honesty as a way of life.*

As important as all the character qualities we have discussed so far, living a life of integrity has to be one of the most important, as it spills over into every area of our lives. Jesus was the epitome of integrity, which we should strive to emulate. We must never get caught up in, or get started with, little white lies. They can seem inconsequential initially and no big deal, but they can quickly become devastating to our relationships. They are habit-forming as one leads to another until it becomes a way of life.

This reminds me of Sir Walter Scott's quote: *"Oh what a tangled web we weave, when first we practice to deceive."* My husband was reminding me that hundreds of times during his FBI career, when called upon to testify in court, he had to answer this question: *"Do you solemnly swear to tell the truth, the whole truth and nothing but the truth, so help you, God?"* If you don't tell the *whole* truth, you are not telling *the* truth. You are telling a lie. Therein lies a very fine line, doesn't it? God "hates" lies and the deception that accompanies them. Jesus described the devil as the "father of lies" (John 8:44). The devil mixed partial truths with lies in tempting Jesus in the desert.

Withholding information is just as devastating and dishonest as lying, leading to resentment and bolder lies. The danger behind it is that the more we lie, the less trustworthy we become. We start trusting others less, which results in damaged relationships. This is something you would never plan, but unfortunately, it results from dishonesty in our lives, which ultimately leads to a breakdown of trust, leading to a failure of respect and self-respect. Rebuilding trust at this point is challenging.

When any of this happens, a person of integrity will make every effort to restore relationships by apologizing, taking responsibility for failures, and requesting forgiveness. At this point, they are recommitting themselves to telling the truth and staying on that path.

When we choose to live by the truth, we love ourselves and others. Even if the truth may sometimes seem to be eclipsed by the darkness of the world, we must remember that truth is the light, and the light can never be extinguished. Darkness cannot overcome even just a flickering flame. The slightest little bit of light will expose what is lurking in the darkness. Where there's truth, there is hope.

God does not expect us to be perfect, but we are to live with integrity as a Christ-follower. What matters is the direction and attitude of our heart. God is more interested in our heart than our sins. We're never going to perfect or sinless, but we can sin less. That is a choice, and it's a choice of integrity. It starts with being honest with God, owning our sin, and confessing it with the desire to do the right thing and walk with God in integrity.

Live honorably, love completely, and choose wisely—choose honesty and live a life of integrity today. God bless, and I'll see you tomorrow!

9/8 Thursday – on route to France via Amsterdam

God,
Please restore a right spirit and provide give me a pure ♡ toward father. Let me be emptied so you can fill me and your beautiful truth can be exposed in me teaching and please do this for all the teachers.
Humility, Pure-heartedness love for you & the women of father for confidence in you
let us get out of the way so your beauty love grace & hope can shine & welcome & bring women close to you.

DAY 20
Choose Vulnerability and Authenticity

What is vulnerability? The dictionary will tell you it's the willingness to show emotion or allow one's weakness to be seen or known. It's a willingness to risk being hurt or attacked. Vulnerability is not weakness. It's emotional risk, exposure, uncertainty, and it fuels our daily lives. It's essentially the most accurate measurement of courage. It's the birthplace of innovation, creativity, accountability and change.

To create is to make something that has never existed before. There is nothing more vulnerable than that. Adaptability to change is all about vulnerability. To be honest, I have felt incredibly vulnerable writing books and putting them "out there" for anyone to read and criticize. The contents reveal my heart, convictions, emotions, and opinions about topics that are very precious to me.

In our culture today, vulnerability and authenticity are regarded as essential attributes but are rarely found. Being vulnerable is both freeing and terrifying. It's freeing in that when we open up and become vulnerable, we invite others to share our emotions so that we are not alone in carrying them. But at the same time, it can be terrifying because those with whom we are sharing may not help us carry those emotions. There may be a disconnect or even criticism or opposition.

Even from a young age, we are taught that it's better to keep any shame and painful memories well hidden. Otherwise, we might experience embarrassment or cause someone to get angry, and sharing probably would not make us feel any better anyway. Whatever the reason, we have embraced the myth that it's best to keep those things close to our chest and avoid being honest and authentic.

Ultimately, we all fear rejection which is probably at the root of the tendency to shun vulnerability and authenticity. I constantly encourage believers to look to Christ as our example on so many levels. Here is another example. Although He never sinned, Jesus would carry the pain of rejection on the cross. Also in John 11:35, when His friend Lazarus died, it says, "Jesus wept." He didn't find the need to hide His true emotions. He was genuine and authentic.

Jesus asks us to be authentic as well. James 5:16 tells us, "Therefore, confess your sins to one another and pray for one another, that you may be healed." There is healing in vulnerability. Sometimes vulnerability is not shared because of shame. The truth is there are three things that shame needs to survive, and they are secrecy, silence, and judgment. But when met with empathy, love, and compassion, shame is destroyed.

When we ask God to examine our hearts, He will reveal where we need to make changes and healing can begin.

Vulnerability is the secret to beautiful growth. Without a willingness to expose ourselves to possible failure, nothing will change. It takes courage and bravery to run after something that might fail, but it's the only way to live a whole-hearted life.

How do we develop the courage to be vulnerable and authentic? We can start by being vulnerable with God. He can certainly handle our pain, questions, fears, and brokenness. He wants to handle it for us.

We need to learn how to be vulnerable with ourselves and permit ourselves to hurt. Even though we know we don't have it all together, we can be vulnerable because we have a Savior. Once we accept ourselves, then we can begin to accept others. Our judgmental feelings will dissipate, and we'll want to reach out to help others.

To love is to be vulnerable. Is it possible that without being vulnerable and authentic, we are only living half-hearted lives? God is calling us to be vulnerable with Him and genuine with each other. Getting to that point is one of the bravest things we can ever accomplish. It's not something we do naturally in our own strength. It's a complete paradigm shift. Vulnerability goes against our culture. By making ourselves vulnerable, we risk getting hurt. However, the alternative is becoming hardened and unbreakable. In other words, we will become robots, incapable of experiencing the love or joy God intended us to share.

We can look to King David in the Bible for an example of vulnerability and authenticity. He made some huge mistakes in his life, and He knew that God knew everything about him, and yet he prayed in Psalm 139:23-24, "Search me, O God, and know my heart! Try me and know my thoughts! And see if there be any grievous way in me, and lead me in the way everlasting!"

Our best step often comes on the other side of a vulnerable prayer. When we ask God to examine our hearts, He will reveal where we need to make changes and healing can begin. His goal is not to condemn us but to give us a joy-filled life. When we stop feeling like we have to impress God, we can start being changed by Him.

Live honorably, love completely, and choose wisely—choose to be vulnerable and authentic today. God bless, and I'll see you tomorrow!

DAY 21
Choose Contentment

Do you sometimes find yourself lacking contentment? What is contentment, and what does it mean to be content in any situation? Is that even possible? Dictionary.com tells us that to be content, we are satisfied with what we have, not wanting anything else.

Learning to be content in any situation begins with understanding the difference between being happy and being content. They are not synonymous. We can be happy without being content, and we can be content without being happy. What do I mean?

Have you ever met someone who exudes calm, peace, and contentment even though they live with limitations or aliments that are difficult and painful? Perhaps they have even faced a heart-wrenching tragedy in the past. Yet, they seem so in control, so serene in their faith, actually even appear joyful on every level? This is someone who has learned the art of contentment.

Happiness is an emotion, whereas contentment is a state of being. We can be happy today and unhappy tomorrow, depending on circumstances. No matter our circumstances, being content certainly seems to be counter-cultural and counter-intuitive, doesn't it? It means we can give our problems or concerns to God and leave them there. It's learning how to "let go and let God."

Our best model for that is Paul in the New Testament. Here is a guy who met Jesus in a vision on the road to Damascus, where he was on his way to persecute the "Christ-followers" of his day. (See Acts 9 for that amazing story.) After that, he renounced all he had, took on a Christ-follower mission that resulted in his being homeless, beaten within an inch of his life several times, even left for dead once, shipwrecked, and imprisoned numerous times. Yet he said he had learned to be content whatever his circumstances because he served the living Christ, and that was all that mattered to him.

Contentment is a learned behavior. We are not born with it, and it doesn't come easy for anyone. But by God's grace, as we grow in our relationship with Him, we mature, and we can learn how to make contentment a way of life.

Paul tells us in Philippians 4:11-13, "Not that I am speaking of being in need, for I have learned in whatever situation I am to be content. I know how to be brought low, and I know how to abound. In any and every circumstance, I have learned the secret of facing plenty and hunger, abundance, and need. I can do all things through Him who strengthens me."

Happiness is an emotion, whereas contentment is a state of being and is a learned behavior.

I have heard so many people say, "If this or that happens, then I'll be happy." It's all based on circumstances. Once they get the coveted achievement, then I so often hear something like, "That's it? Is that all there is?" Jim Carey, the comedic celebrity, once said, "I think everybody should get rich and famous and do everything they ever dreamed of so they can see that it's not the answer."

I heard of a reporter who interviewed Muhammed Ali at his farmhouse, and Ali gave the reporter a tour. They ended up in his barn, where all his trophies, ribbons, and memorabilia were showcased on the shelves gathering dust and even pigeon droppings. Ali softly said, "I had the world, I had all the world, and it was nothin'." I often think we place too much importance on what other people think of us rather than what God thinks. Who really should matter in the long run?

Paul tells us earlier in the same chapter to be anxious for nothing, but we are to go to God in prayer with our needs with thanksgiving. The book of Philippians is a letter he wrote to the congregation of a church he had started in Philippi, Greece. It has become known as "the epistle of joy" because he keeps referring to the joy of the Lord as his strength, giving him peace. Paul wrote this letter when he was in prison, so I would say he had mastered what it was like to rest in Jesus, who gave him the peace and joy he could never have experienced without learning how to be content whatever his circumstances.

Learning contentment is not inevitable. Many of us know someone who has gotten trapped in their suffering long ago, turned inward and became an angry, resentful person.

None of us can avoid some level of pain or hardship during our lifetime. My prayer is that when faced with some sort of turmoil in your life, you will remember Paul and learn as he did, that when anchored in Christ, the fruit of contentment is developed when we are thankful for what God has provided whether we like it or not. By expressing gratitude, Paul experienced the richness of being, not having. The truth is, we don't have to like where we are or what we have. Still, if we will choose to thank God for His provisions regardless of our feelings toward them, we'll experience the same contentment as Paul.

Live honorably, love completely, and choose wisely—choose contentment today. God bless, and I'll see you tomorrow!

DAY 22
Choose Generosity

Wikipedia defines generosity as "The habit of giving freely without expecting anything in return. It can involve offering time, assets, or talents to aid someone in need. Often equated with the virtue of charity, generosity is widely accepted in society as a desirable trait." That definition is not incorrect but needs to be expanded to include the fact that generosity is an attitude and a spirit of awareness of opportunities to wholeheartedly, extravagantly share what we have with others showing empathy, transparency, and compassion. Generosity requires sacrifice and a change in perspective.

As busy as we all are today, giving the gift of time is colossal and a great demonstration of generosity. Time is so precious that when given, it is a powerful expression of love. There never seems to be enough time to do all that we strive to do, but no matter our income, status, or abilities, we all have the same amount of time (24 hours a day, 168 hours per week, 8760 hours per year). It is so easy for our time to be eaten up by all kinds of inconsequential things unless we intentionally determine to be careful about how we spend it.

We tend to take the time to do what is most important to us, so giving up our time to be with someone to do what they want to do is a real sign of care and generosity. One can always make more money, but time can never be redeemed. Once it's gone, it's gone, so sharing your time is being extremely generous.

Giving of one's talents by using their skills to meet someone's needs is another expression of love through generosity. Still, the giving of money seems to be the most well-known and understood example of being generous. Our goal in making money should never be an end unto itself. We should strive to make enough money, not only to meet our needs and that of our family, but also the needs of others. We must keep in mind that money, like everything else we have in life, is a gift. The joy we receive in using it to bless others cannot be measured and is just one of life's benefits.

Some people have the mentality that, "When I start making more money," or "when I make a certain amount of money," then I'll give a portion of it away." They may actually believe that, but few ever reach that point. As the author, W.S. Plumer wrote, "He who is not liberal with what he has, does but deceive himself when he thinks he would be liberal if he had more." In other words, because generosity is an attitude, if we don't give a little when we have a little, we won't be inclined to give even a little when we have much.

The joy that comes from giving far exceeds the sacrifice of doing so.

With this mentality, the more one makes, the greedier they become. If our hearts focus on ourselves, then we seek to accumulate all the wealth we can for ourselves. In contrast, if we focus on others, we will want to invest all we can in our relationships.

It doesn't matter how much we give as long as it is with a generous spirit. The joy that comes from giving far exceeds the sacrifice of doing so. You probably have heard that you cannot out-give God. I'm sure you've also heard that it's in giving that we receive. Both are so true. When you have a generous spirit motivated by love and give freely and sacrificially, it will not only produce joy but will flow back to you multiplied. There seems to be an unwritten law of nature that giving attracts abundance. However, we need to be sure that we are giving with the right attitude, for the sake of relationships and meeting others' needs, rather than to receive praise and recognition or any return from our generosity.

A truly generous person has learned to keep in perspective the importance of earthly possessions and not give them more priority than they should. Winston Churchill once said, "We make a living by what we earn; we make a life by what we give." When we can truly learn the art of giving, we understand the art of living and find that we have more than we ever realized. When we give out of a heart of love rather than duty, we experience a spirit of gratitude rather than pride in our giving. It is said that God loves a cheerful giver.

Giving away your resources, whether it be your time, talents, or money in any relationship, can be a thankless act. The important thing is that you maintain a generous attitude. Even if no one acknowledges your generosity, you will have grown into a more loving individual and will be rewarded. Remember, we reap what we sow.

When we become more generous with our time, talents, and money, it affects every area of our lives. The best way I know to get the most out of life is to give yourself away.

Live honorably, love completely, and choose wisely—choose to be generous today. God bless, and I'll see you tomorrow!

DAY 23
Choose Fellowship

There is no way we can live out our Christian life in isolation. To quote John Donne, "No man is an island." People need people, and some more than others.

We were created for fellowship, first with God and then with each other. I like to think of fellowship as a mutual bond that Christians have with Christ, which puts us in a deep, eternal relationship with Him and one another. Christian fellowship is a profound awareness of a lasting relationship of love among the brethren.

Many of us are involved in relationships with numerous people. Still, there are a few of us who experience something more profound. We call it fellowship. There's an excellent reason we refer to other Christians as brothers and sisters. The kinship we share with our fellow heirs in Christ is more deeply rooted than any physical bloodline or familial tie.

I am reminded of 1 Thessalonians 2:8, where Paul says, "So, being affectionately desirous of you, we were ready to share with you not only the gospel of God but also our own selves, because you had become very dear to us."

This fellowship is an essential part of our faith. Coming together to support one another is an

There is no way we can live out our Christian life in isolation.

experience that allows us to learn, gain strength, and show the world precisely who God is.

So what are the benefits of fellowship? I'll give you five:

1. Fellowship Gives Us a Picture of God

Each of us together shows all of God's graces to the world. No one is perfect. We all sin, but each of us has a purpose here on earth to show aspects of God to those around us. Each of us has been given specific spiritual gifts. When we come together in fellowship, it's like us as a whole demonstrating God. Think of it like a cake. You need flour, sugar, eggs, oil, and more to make a cake. The eggs will never be the flour. None of them make up the cake alone. Yet together, all those ingredients make a delicious cake. It is like that with fellowship. All of us together show the glory of God.

2. Fellowship Makes us Stronger

Being around other believers gives us the chance to learn and grow in our faith. It demonstrates to us why we believe and sometimes is the excellent nourishment needed for our souls. It's always good to spend some time in fellowship so that we remember that it is God who makes us strong.

3. Fellowship Provides Encouragement

We all are prone to have bad moments in which we may find ourselves discouraged. If we get too low, it can lead to anger and a feeling of disillusionment with God. These difficult times are why fellowship is so important. Spending time with other believers can often lift us up. They help us to keep our eyes on God and He often uses them to provide what we need in dark times. Coming together with others can aid in our healing process and give us the encouragement to move forward. (Hebrews 10:25)

4. Fellowship Reminds Us We Are Not Alone

God wants us to come together so that we always know we're not alone. Fellowship allows us to build those lasting relationships so we're never by ourselves in the world. It's amazing that no matter where you may find yourself in the world, when you meet another believer, there is an instant bond and you suddenly feel at home.

5. Fellowship Helps Us Grow

When we come together in fellowship, we teach each other things. God gives us a gift of learning and growing as we read our Bibles and pray together. When we come alongside one another in fellowship, we show each other how to live as God wants us to live, and how to walk in His footsteps.

If you are not already in a small group of likeminded individuals with whom you can be vulnerable and share, my call of action would be for you to look at joining or starting such a group where you can be transparent and be willing to give as much as you take.

I'll close with this from 1 Thessalonians 5:11, "Therefore encourage one another and build one another up, just as you are doing."

Live honorably, love completely, and choose wisely—choose to be in fellowship today. God bless, and I'll see you tomorrow!

DAY 24
Choose Prayer

I'm no expert, and there is so much that could be said about prayer, but I will be sharing my best practices here when it comes to prayer. My recommendation—get up early. There is no better way to start your day than time with the Lord. It's starting your day with the right mindset, so that when difficulties face you that day—and they will, you will be much better equipped to respond in a godly way than if you had not spent time clothing yourself with the humility of Christ, asking for His guidance and wisdom, developing an attitude of gratitude, and putting on the armor of God.

Also, at least I've found that if I don't start my day with prayer, life will soon get in the way, and there's a good chance I never will get to it. Having it scheduled as a habit works best for me.

If it helps, make an appointment with God. Visualize Him sitting by the fireplace waiting for you each morning at an appointed time, or wherever it is that you can get alone by yourself, preferably where you can talk to Him out loud. If you know He is waiting for you, you're not going to evade God because you stayed up watching mindless late-night TV, are you? You might want to grab a cup of coffee first if you need it to stay awake. I have found that I need to pray out loud; otherwise, my mind will wander, and I might fight sleep, so talking to Him with my voice keeps my mind on track.

I am not a journaler, but I highly recommend that for many reasons. For one thing, it keeps your mind focused. You can write down your concerns and requests with a date, and later on, when your prayers are answered, you can go back and document it with a date. Later you can go back and be reminded of God's faithfulness; otherwise, we tend to forget these things. Also, after you're gone, your family will be encouraged when they read your journal to see your faith and the faithfulness of God.

There's no better way to start your day than talking with God to get your focus on Him and get guidance for the day. If you want to hear from God, you must be still and quiet after asking Him what He wants to tell you. This is so important and the most challenging part—being still and just listening. Please don't see your prayer time with God as an obligation that you should do. You are not checking off a box! What a privilege it is to have direct access to the Creator of the universe, knowing that He hears you and is delighted to spend time with you. Do you realize what an honor that is?

I have found the best way to pray is to start with a form of worship of praise and adoration. Maybe play some worship songs. That's what I do while I shower and get dressed for my day. Then I praise Him for some of His attributes that mean so much to me. I put a list of many of His amazing attributes at the end of this book you can use as a guide, along with an explanation of each and a Bible verse to go along with each one. This is not an exhaustive list, but it's pretty comprehensive.

> *Prayer in no way changes God's mind, but it changes us as we see Him at work, and He invites us to join Him in what He is doing.*

Then I ask the Lord to show me areas of my life I need to confess so I can start the day with a clean slate, and then I confess any known sin. Then I thank Him for His many blessings that I continually enjoy or answers to prayers. Then I pray for myself and intercede for others. This form of prayer is called **ACTS**: It's an acronym for **A**doration, **C**onfession, **T**hanksgiving, and **S**upplication. This just gives prayer time some structure. It's not a formula or a "must" way of praying it is just one way we can communicate on a deep level and is helpful if you feel you need structure.

For me, even though the Holy Spirit lives within me, I think it's beneficial also to ask Him to fill me and make me aware of His presence each day, to guide and direct my day, so that I am led to spend time on things that are important and not waste time that cannot be redeemed.

Scripture tells us that God wants us to pray for Him to meet our needs, but most importantly, if we we're going to see the power of prayer, we must take our eyes off ourselves and focus our prayers on the needs of others. Then we will truly see the power of God in our lives and our prayers. Praying that God will be glorified in a situation always aligns with His will.

Remember that prayer is just a conversation with God—a two-way conversation, so we need to take time to listen as well as speak. He will respond in your mind, giving you ideas. At the same time, we must remember that God's timing is perfect, and He doesn't always respond on our timetable, so we must be willing to wait for His timing when it comes to answering our prayers.

Prayer in no way changes God's mind, but it changes us as we see Him at work, and He invites us to join Him in what He is doing.

I should add that prayer is not just a morning activity; although concentrated, deliberate time is essential. We are commanded in Scripture in 1 Thessalonians 5:17 to pray without ceasing, so we should remain in a prayerful state throughout the day. It just starts with a quiet time in the morning. Scripture tells us that Jesus often slipped away to pray. If we are to model Him, we should do the same. James reminds us in his first chapter that we must pray in faith, believing God will hear and answer our prayers. Why does God want us to pray? Among many reasons, all for our benefit, He wants us to learn to trust Him. He also knows that we miss the many gifts He has planned for us when we fail to get with Him. Remember, we are only as close to God as we choose to be.

Live honorably, love completely, and choose wisely—choose to pray today and every day. God bless, and I'll see you tomorrow.

Interesting as I read This book God seems to be preparing my heart to receive The specific message and tract. last night I really dreamt about doing a big service project for the Norris.

DAY 25
Choose Service

As always, we can look to Jesus as our perfect model and greatest example of selflessness. In Mark 10:45 it says, "For even the Son of Man came not to be served but to serve others and to give His life as a ransom for many."

What are some valuable lessons we can learn from Him? Here are just a few:

- Consider the needs of others.
- Serve generously and without reservation
- Serve with gladness

There are all kinds of opportunities around us in which we can be the hands and feet of Christ to serve others. Sometimes, all it takes is showing some kindness and courtesy, taking our focus off ourselves, and looking out for others' needs. God didn't put us here just to live for ourselves. He wants us to leave our little corner of the world a better place than we found it. One of the best ways we do that and serve God is by serving others.

Depending on the translation, there are around 58 times in the Bible that the phrase "one another" can be found. "Love one another." Care for one another." "Pray for one another." "Help one another." "Support one another." Encourage one another." And so on—the list goes on and on.

That is how it is supposed to be in the family of God. God meant for us to look for ways to serve one another.

No question, there will be times when it is not easy. It may mean sacrifice. It may mean serving a problematic person. If you do get discouraged by doing good in this way and probably will at some point, we need to remember a couple of things.

1. There is a reward awaiting you for your obedience in this area. Hebrews 6:10 states: "God is not unjust; He will not forget your work and the love you have shown Him as you have helped His people and continue to help them."

2. Nothing we do for God is insignificant or done in vain. Paul tells us in 1 Corinthians 15:58: " Therefore, my beloved brothers, be steadfast, immovable, always abounding in the work of the Lord, knowing that in the Lord your labor is not in vain."

Let's talk about some of the benefits and blessings that come out of service to others.

1. As you serve, you might uncover and discover a spiritual gift you never knew you had if you had not exercised it.

2. You might experience or witness a miracle.

3. Serving allows us to experience the joy and peace that comes from obedience.

4. As we shift our focus from ourselves to others, we become more like Jesus.

5. Serving side-by-side with other believers forms bonds and relationships with like-minded individuals, helping us spur one another to love and good deeds.

6. Inevitably, when we step out of our comfort zones to serve others, it increases our faith.

7. Serving others gives us the opportunity to build our faith and experience God's presence in new ways. As we encourage others and they find healing, we are encouraged as well.

8. When we take our eyes off ourselves to serve others, meeting their needs, it is therapeutic to ease our symptoms of stress and depression. It can be the best distraction from our worries, replacing that with a "feel good" hormone dopamine released when doing good.

I used to be very selfish with my time because I knew that once it was gone, it was gone and I would never get it back. That was before I learned what a blessing it was to pour into and be a part of other people's lives and what value it added to mine. So when you give your time in service to others, it truly is a gift. God will bless you for that.

There may be numerous reasons you think you don't have what it takes to serve in a particular way. You may feel like you don't have anything to offer. Just remember that God doesn't call the equipped; He equips the called. He would not call you to do something without faithfully enabling you to do it.

God used many simple and the most unsuspecting people in Scripture to do amazing things for His kingdom and glory because He was in it. God doesn't just want to work through but in you. In fact, He may have to do a work *in* you before He can work *through* you. In any case, you come out the winner!

> *God would not call you to do something without faithfully enabling you to do it.*

Live honorably, love completely, and choose wisely—choose service today. God bless, and I'll see you tomorrow!

DAY 26
Choose to Seek Godly Wisdom

What is wisdom? Proverbs 9:10 tells us, "The fear of the Lord is the beginning of wisdom." This refers to reverencing God for who He is. Wisdom is seeing things from God's viewpoint and responding to them according to His Word. Knowledge and wisdom are not the same. One can know a lot and not be wise. Knowledge without wisdom is insufficient. Wisdom is discerning—knowing what to do with the knowledge we have. In biblical terms, it's putting biblical principles into practice. God will give us wisdom if we are willing to act on it.

When comparing the wisdom of God with the wisdom of the world, the world's wisdom is foolishness in comparison because God is left out of the equation. We can only have godly wisdom when following His instructions, as pointed out in His Word. Wisdom is the ability to perceive what is truly going on in a situation and then implementing God's will regarding that knowledge. To know the will of God is the highest of all wisdom.

The Proverbs are full of verses that talk about wisdom. It is often referred to it as the book of wisdom. King Solomon, who wrote Proverbs, sought godly wisdom, and so should we. Here is another important Proverb: 13:20, "Whoever walks with the wise becomes wise, but the companion of fools will suffer harm." This infers that we should hang out with wise people. Before we leave Proverbs, I must share my life verse, Proverbs 3: 5-6, " Trust in the LORD with all your heart, and do not lean on your own understanding. In all your ways acknowledge Him, and He will make straight your paths."

So, how do we get godly wisdom? The only way we can learn it is through prayer and by the study of His Word. Prayer only works if we are quiet long enough to listen and hear His instruction. The Bible was given to us for instruction in the ways of God. It is our life's manual. If we don't read it, how can we know God's wisdom or His purpose or will for our life?

Recognizing my need for God's wisdom, I have included in my daily quiet time to ask Him for His wisdom as I go about my day. In the Good News Translation, James 1:5 says, "But if any of you lacks wisdom, you should pray to God, who will give it to you; because God gives generously and graciously to all." All we have to do is to ask for it in faith, believing He will give it.

I'm sure you would concur that life is full of twists and turns, of detours and drop-offs, resulting in us constantly having to make decisions. We need the wisdom to discern what is going on to do the right thing (to make the right choices) with that information.

Knowledge may help you make a living. Wisdom leads to a godly life.

First, we have to know what is valid in all the rhetoric thrown at us every day. The only way to know what is true is to know what God's Word says. Once we know the facts, then we need to know what to do with it. That is what we call understanding.

If I can be cute for a minute—when knowledge gets married to understanding, then we have a baby called wisdom. Godly wisdom is so valuable that it is hidden in God, and we must dig for it. It is not easily accessible for just anyone. Proverbs 3:13-14 says, " Blessed is the one who finds wisdom, and the one who gets understanding, for the gain from her is better than gain from silver and her profit better than gold."

For the last sixteen years or so, my husband and I have been mentoring married couples struggling in their marriages. Often, a couple's issues appear to be far above our pay grade. While we attempt to give them godly advice based on Scripture and our personal experience, sometimes we think it wise to recommend they also see a professional counselor. While we can coach, we are not trained as counselors.

We always highly recommend that they only seek out a Christian counselor because while two people may get training from the same prestigious school and hold the same degrees, the Christian counselor will benefit from godly wisdom to apply to their knowledge and advice. They will have a godly perception, discernment, and spiritual insight lacking in a secular counselor, because those things are spiritual in nature. True wisdom only comes from God.

We need to learn how to recognize what is important and what is not. We make every decision based on our values, so we need to clarify those—where did they come from? What is most beneficial? That comes through wisdom. Our values in life will dictate our stress, our success, and our salvation.

How do we know that we fear God—revere Him for who He is? It's when we obey even when it's not something we prefer to do—even when it doesn't appear to be to our advantage to do so. We recognize and acknowledge that His ways often not our ways or His thoughts like our thoughts. (Isaiah 55:8) We personify our fear, our awe of the Lord when we obey regardless of our feelings.

Wisdom seeks understanding, not a need to be right. And above all else, it seeks to lift God's Kingdom here on Earth. Being knowledgeable can be a blessing, but being wise is the greater blessing. Knowledge may help you make a living. Wisdom leads to a godly life.

Live honorably, love completely, and choose wisely—choose to pray for God's wisdom and understanding. God bless, and I will see you tomorrow.

DAY 27
Choose Surrender and Obedience

Surrender and obedience—wow, this is a topic I am very passionate about because God has been teaching me so much about this in my own life over the last several years. He had been after me to write a book about this, and I resisted. I don't know why I thought I could strong-arm God, but that is precisely what I did for so long.

He taught me so much about obedient surrender and its benefits, and I felt led to write a book about it but had so many limiting beliefs that I resisted for the longest time. I knew this idea had to come from the Lord because—for one thing, I don't like to write. It's not something that comes naturally to me, at least as a desire. I don't journal, and I wouldn't say I even like to take notes.

I'm just a no-name nobody anyway. Who would ever read a book by me? No one knows who and am, and why would I be qualified to write such a book? Why would they waste their time and money on a book like that after I would have spent months writing it?

Well, He finally convinced me that I didn't need to know how He was going to use it. I just needed to be obedient and do it. So I did, and it actually didn't take that long because He inspired me and the words flowed once I got started. I learned that He often wants to guide and direct us, but He can only do that if we are already in motion—moving forward. I just had to take that first step.

I still didn't know how He would use it, but I knew it would be an excellent exercise because of what I would learn from it. Of course, that turned out to be true. He even turned what I thought was going to be one book into three before He inspired me to write this one. I still have three more in my head and heart that I believe He will help me to get into print over the next year.

I cannot tell you how freeing and empowering it is to respond to God's call with obedience. I still feel very insignificant but have gained tons of confidence and feel so much closer to God. Once I responded with obedience and surrendered my limiting beliefs to His direction, I have to pay it forward. I am not to keep these biblically-based lessons to myself when there are so many people who also struggle in the area of surrender and obedience.

I felt compelled to write that book because while working with married couples in a marriage enrichment program at our church, and after mentoring married couples with my husband for the past 16 years, we have seen the core problem in these marriages. It is basically a lack of understanding that it is in the surrendered life, the obedient life, the crucified life that we experience the victorious, abundant life. It's a failure to apply all these attributes that are covered in this short devotional.

> *The victorious Christian life is lived, by faith, in a moment-by-moment surrender and obedience to God.*

We hear and believe in our head that it is in giving that we receive, but for some reason, when it comes to marriage, it becomes all about "me." "You aren't meeting my needs. You are supposed to make me happy," and so on. We forget about the importance of putting our spouse's needs before our own and serving them. It's hard when affirming words or actions of service are not being reciprocated and we feel unloved or disrespected. This mindset can leak over into any relationship. This has just been my observation and experience in mentoring couples.

As Christ-followers, our goal is to be like Christ. What do we see when we look at Christ? We see absolute surrender to God. He modeled for us the ultimate example of a surrendered life. That was the very root of His life. In the Garden of Gethsemane, He prayed, "Your will be done" (Matthew 26:42). The apostle John quoted Him in 4:34: "My food is to do the will of Him who sent me and to accomplish His work." Then in 6:38, He said, "For I have come down to from heaven, not to do my own will but the will of Him who sent me."

The theme of the book I wrote and referenced earlier is Galatians 2:20, where Paul says, I have been crucified with Christ. It is no longer I who live, but Christ who lives in me. And the life I now live in the flesh I live by faith in the Son of God, who loved me and gave Himself for me."

The victorious Christian life is lived, by faith, in a moment-by-moment surrender and obedience to God. It is a life rooted and grounded in faith and surrender. True saving faith produces obedience and submission to the Lordship of Jesus Christ—the only thing that fills the God-shaped vacuum in our lives. It results in rewards we would not otherwise experience. One thing for sure—the victorious life is not is a mirage. It certainly is obtainable, sustainable, and eternal. It comes through surrender and learned through obedience.

Nothing brings greater joy to a Christ-follower than knowing they are fully surrendered and walking in obedience to the Lordship of Christ.

Live honorably, love completely, and choose wisely—choose surrender and obedience today. God bless, and I'll see you tomorrow

DAY 28
Choose Praise and Worship

Just as we learned about gratitude, our choices make a huge difference in how we view our life and circumstances. Are you under stress right now? The best stress buster I'm aware of is worship and praise.

When stressed or depressed, we must turn our focus off ourselves and on to Christ. God has given us a garment of praise for a spirit of heaviness (Isaiah 61:3 - KJV). When we allow worry and anxiety to control us, it robs us of our ability to worship or experience any amount of gratitude.

God made us to worship Him and bring Him pleasure. He is so pleased when we worship Him with a good heart. When we "put on" a spirit of praise, glorifying God for who He is, the spirit of heaviness will leave. Satan cannot exist where God reigns.

Worship is giving God the best that He has given us. We must be careful what we do with the best we have. Whenever we get a blessing from God, we must give it back to Him as a love-gift. Take time to meditate before God and offer the blessing back to Him in a deliberate act of worship.

While it's fine to worship God in a spirit of thanksgiving for what He has done, the primary purpose is to praise Him for who He is. Who is He? He is love. How did He demonstrate His love? By sending His Son to die in our place, bringing us salvation. If He had not done that, we would have no reason to praise Him.

Worship can turn the most miserable circumstances into a beautiful experience. It's a way of putting our faith over our circumstances and honoring God, no matter what we are going through. Worshiping and praising God may or may not result in solving our problems right away. Still, it has a way of making them less significant—not because they have disappeared, but because they have been given a new perspective when observed through a spirit of submission.

There is nothing quite like experiencing the presence of Jesus. Of course, as a Christ-follower, He is always with us and is in us. Still, when we worship Him, adoring and praising Him for who He is and all His many wonderful attributes, it just does something supernatural in our spirit and our soul, providing an amazing intimacy with Him that is extra special and precious, wouldn't you say?

I know for me, it gives me a "shot in the arm" to start my day. I feel empowered by His Spirit to accomplish anything that comes my way. Remember, He wants us to come to Him as we are—not all polished and put together. He does that for us when we yield to Him through our worship.

Our enthusiasm (or lack thereof) to worship is a good barometer of our spiritual condition.

The word worship comes from an old English word that means "worthship." We worship God because He is worthy. It doesn't matter how low we may be feeling or negative our circumstances might be; God merits our worship. Psalm 118:1 says, "Oh give thanks to the LORD, for He is good; for His steadfast love endures forever!"

If you need help to get started with praise, look through the Psalms, which is full of praise. Some of them begin with a lament, as the psalmist

116

often pours out his heart to God in agony over his present circumstances but most end up in praise as he learns to trust God.

Is daily worship a priority for you? Our enthusiasm (or lack thereof) to worship is a good barometer of our spiritual condition. By the way, we don't have to feel like worshiping God to do it. We just NEED to do it. Believe me, it is for our good and benefit. If you're struggling with that, it's okay to pour out your concerns to Him. He already knows the condition of your heart and wants more than anything for you to come clean with Him so He can bless you.

While taking specific time every day to worship God is a beautiful habit to adapt, worship and praise should be a state of being—a way of life. When it is, then when tragedy or a difficult circumstance arises, you are much more equipped to handle it. Those are some of the best opportunities we have to honor God in and through our worship.

When we reach the end of ourselves, He can take over through our worship. Our weakness is made perfect in His strength. Be it in song, prayer, crying out to Him, reading His Word, or soaking up His presence, do whatever it is that gets you into a place where you are reliant and focused on Him. It is impossible to do this based on a feeling or gauged by emotion. The act of choosing to magnify God's name and declaring His goodness and mercy and His love in these times is worship personified. When you choose to command your soul to praise and worship Him, especially during difficult times, you've experienced a breakthrough.

This is much easier said than done, I realize, but your call to action:

Live honorably, love completely, and choose wisely—whatever your circumstances, choose to worship and praise God today. God bless, and I'll see you tomorrow!

DAY 29
Choose a Christ-Centered Life

You know, all of these many devotionals boil down to the theme of living a Christ-centered life. That is our goal as a Christ-follower, is it not? Second Corinthians 5:14-15 says, "For the love of Christ controls us, because we have concluded this: that one has died for all, therefore all have died; and He died for all, that those who live might no longer live for themselves but for Him who for their sake died and was raised." How would you respond if someone asked you if your life centered around Christ?

A Christ-centered life is often equated with going to church, giving, Bible study, prayer, and maybe even sharing our faith. These are all good things. However, suppose our heart is not in it, and our motives are self-centered. In that case, these "religious activities" can be done for many reasons that have nothing to do with our love for Jesus. We could be checking off a box, seeking others' approval, maybe seeking to relieve feelings of guilt or make ourselves feel better, or to look more righteous. We may be concentrating on finding verses that affirm us in our Bible study, and our prayer life might be focused on what we can get from God or get Him to do for us.

If any of this sounds familiar, realize you are not alone. We are fallen human beings who will always struggle with our motives and such. The enemy is always at work to sabotage our hearts and turn our focus inward rather than on Christ and what He desires from us. This internal battle within ourselves will continue as long we live in these earthly bodies. That's why Paul in Ephesians 4:22, 24 tells us to "lay aside the old self, which is being corrupted," and to "put on the new self, which in the likeness of God has been created in righteousness and holiness of the truth."

Do you struggle with limiting beliefs about "not being enough?" The enemy will do whatever it takes to make those who desire to be like Jesus to feel unworthy and keep us from being confident that our identity is in Christ. We must pray for God to remove all false thinking and replace it with His truth. Imagine being able to rise above our worldly thought patterns to view our world and circumstances as Christ does. Though we cannot know all He does, Scripture tells us that once we accept His free gift of salvation, we are given the mind of Christ.

This gives us the ability to maintain the same focus and values He has, and see the world through a Christ-centered lens. This is a gift given to every believer, but it must be developed to experience its full value. We do this by taking our thoughts captive, reading, memorizing and meditating on Scripture, as well as spending consistent time in the presence of Christ and the fellowship of like-minded believers who hold us accountable. We tend to become a lot like the people we spend time with, so we need to choose our friends wisely. Just think of how our lives might change if we spend a lot of time with Christ! As my former pastor, Lon Solomon, used to say, "Not a sermon, just a thought."

If we stay deeply connected with Christ, we can start to view the world through a Christ-centered lens.

To think like Christ does not come naturally. Our natural bent is for our thoughts to be contrary to the things of God. We often set our minds

earthly

on early things because we forget who we serve. We must counter our lives with truth and live intentionally to develop the mind of Christ. Otherwise, in light of our current worldly situations, we will be prone to fear, anxiety, depression, discouragement, and even isolation. But if we stay deeply connected with Christ, we can start to view the world through a Christ-centered lens.

A Christ-centered life is fueled by love for the Savior, which flows and grows as we increase in our knowledge of Him and experience His work in our life. As we learn to know Jesus more intimately through prayer, studying His Word, and quietly abiding in His presence, He will grow in stature in our heart and soul. We'll discover that our self-focus deceases, and He will become the delight of our lives. I have found that the more time I spend in prayer and studying His Word, the more I develop an insatiable appetite for more!

Live honorably, love completely, and choose wisely—choose to develop the mind of Christ and live a Christ-centered life today. God bless, and I'll see you tomorrow!

DAY 30
Choose to Put God First

There are so many things in life that clamor for our attention and devotion, aren't there? Life can get so busy. If we're not careful, it can careen out of control. It's easy to let our career, spouse, kids, friends, even our ministry become more significant than our relationship with God. While these other things are important, there is *nothing* more important than our relationship with God.

If we are not careful, these other things can become idols in our life. What is Idolatry? It's anything we might put in place of God regarding the priority of our attention and affections. When we put the design of our desires before the Designer, that also is idolatry. He must come first. If we are putting anything before our love for God, that's idolatry, which hinders our walk. God must be our first love. In Exodus 20:3, we are commanded: "You shall have no other gods before me."

How many of the things that occupy our time, money, thoughts, energy, and attention have taken the place where God is supposed to be?

Proverbs 3:6 states, "In all your ways acknowledge Him, and He will make straight your paths." This means that if we put God first before our jobs and family life, He will bless us .

The key to having God's abundant life—His love, peace, and joy—is keeping Him in His rightful place in our priorities. That happens only if we intentionally, habitually walk with Him, living for Him. How do we do this? By establishing daily habits of prayer, worship, and regular, consistent time in His Word.

There are so many benefits of keeping God first. Rather than looking to others for validation, make it your goal to have a deep, intimate relationship with God by letting Him into every area of your life. God loves you as much right now as He ever will, and there is nothing you can do to earn or diminish that love. Love is Who God is. Our lives should reflect that. As we live to please God out of our gratefulness for that unconditional love, He promises to bless our lives and make us prosper. See 1 Thessalonians 2:4.

When you decide to love and serve God with your whole heart and make Him first in your life, your soul will prosper, and your joy and peace will increase.

> *When Christ becomes the first place in your heart, you will experience victory—an abundant life—the life you always wanted.*

Remember to lean on Him more than anything else and tell Him, "God, I want to do this, but I can't do it without You." He doesn't expect you to live for Him relying only on your strength or ability, and He understands when you make mistakes.

So if you mess up, don't be discouraged and let it hold you back; confess it and keep going. God will give you the grace to do what you need to do. One day at a time, you and God together can do anything! He so wants to do life with you.

A Christ-follower's life should be characterized by a moment-by-moment surrender to God, which will result in His love flowing through us like a conduit to others, drawing them to Him. Our life and how we conduct ourselves should demonstrate whose we are. We must remember as well that everything good we experience in life is a gift from God. Certainly, He deserves first place in our heart and all our devotion.

If you haven't already done so, it is my prayer that you will fall in love with Jesus as I have. If you make Him the priority in your life and learn to make Him Lord as well as Savior, you will experience the abundant, empowered life. When Christ becomes the first place in your heart, you will experience victory—an abundant life—the life you always wanted.

One of my favorite verses related to this is one I have chosen to have framed on my desk. It is from Matthew 6:33 in the New Living Translation, "Seek the Kingdom of God above all else and live righteously, and He will give you everything you need." It's so important to keep the main thing the main thing.

If this month only has 30 days, don't skip Day 31. I saved one of the best for last, so be sure to check out day 31!

Live honorably, love completely, and choose wisely— choose to put God first not just today, but always. God bless, and I'll see you tomorrow.

DAY 31
Choose to Finish Well

Have you thought much about the end of your life and how you are leaving your little corner of the world? Are you making a positive eternal impact? Are you living a life that others want to emulate? Are you living your life in such a way that others say, I want to have that kind of impact in the lives of others? These are thoughtful questions, aren't they? These questions cross my mind every time I attend a memorial service.

Has God given you a job to do? In everything we do, whether we choose it or not, there is a finish point. You know, as lovely as it is to start well, what's much more important is that we end well. That means trusting God's wisdom all the way to the finish line. Even if we don't win or accomplish our goals, we must finish the task before us without giving up. When we do, we will have lived well.

Can you think of two or three best, significant choices you have made in your life? What is one choice you made that you wish you could take back—hit a reset button? There are few gifts we will leave behind to future generations. What are you passing on that matters most?

We can pass along all kind of material wealth through our will—our estate, but if we do that without also passing along the wisdom of what to do with it and how to handle it, we set them up for failure. We must make sure we are teaching by our example how to make wise, godly decisions in all walks of life—about God, relationships, how to deal with adversity, conflict, etc.—all the experiences we encounter in life. The best way I know to finish well is to teach the next generation how to make wise choices.

The writer of Hebrews in 12:1-2 tells us, " Let us also lay aside every weight, and sin which clings so closely, and let us run with endurance the race that is set before us, looking to Jesus, the founder and perfecter of our faith, who for the joy that was set before Him endured the cross, despising the shame, and is seated at the right hand of the throne of God."

We must recognize that life is not a sprint, but a marathon, a long-distance race. It's not so much how we begin but how we finish that matters. It's about perseverance and endurance for the whole length of the course.

Our ultimate model of finishing well is Jesus. He was able to ascend to the Father because He had finished the mission He set out to accomplish. Sometimes it feels like more is coming at us than we can handle. Sometimes we are even hampered by our sin and weaknesses that keep us focused more on ourselves than on God and others. If we quit before it's finished or run defeated to the finish line, we might miss the strength that awaits us. Don't lose heart. The ascended Lord, who has gone before us, will help us to finish well.

It's important to finish well for many reasons. One being that how we finish this assignment might determine our next appointment. While it may be tempting to quit before you've finished with a particular task, may I encourage you to lean into the faithfulness of God and finish well. Remember that whatever is before you—a difficult conversation, a financial limitation, a physical weakness—whatever difficulty you face, God's strength is with you.

> *As lovely as it is to start well, what's much more important is that we end well. That means trusting God's wisdom all the way to the finish line.*

Every assignment or season God calls us to offers an eternal perspective. We can trust Him that He promises restoration, confirmation and strength if we don't give up.

I'm sure we all can think of someone we know who has not finished well. There is no room in a life destined for a godly legacy for there to be unconfessed, habitual sin. If that is a problem, you must tap into the Holy Spirit's power to help overcome it. There is no question we all leave a legacy. The question is, what kind of legacy are we leaving?

Your obedience now will provide a legacy of faithfulness to the next generation. While on the legacy topic, do you realize that when you faithfully, continually pray for someone, your prayers may outlive you and come to fruition years later? Never stop praying. You may pass away, but the impact of your prayers will not.

We only have one opportunity to live this life. What task or calling has God set for you? Something I have said before, God may need to do something in you before He can work through you. We must make sure we are open to the Holy Spirit with a teachable attitude, so we can be an empty vessel to be filled with the Spirit, living a life of surrender and obedience so He can use us to accomplish His plan and purpose.

I urge you not to give up until He says it's complete. In everything we do, whether we choose it or not, there is a finish line, and I know you want to finish well. I know I long to hear at the end of my life, "Well done, good and faithful servant." Remember, other people's opinion of you really shouldn't matter. We should be living out our life to an audience of only one—Jesus. He is the only one who knows everything about you and still loves you completely. It is He who establishes your identity as a child of God.

What have you started that you need to finish? What commitments have you made that you need to complete? Only what's done for Christ will last, and He is the only one who can give you eternal rewards for a life well-lived.

There are so many attributes and character traits we could discuss. But I have chosen some that have been the most transformative to me. I felt I could share these with authenticity because of my personal experience. This is our last devotion in this series. I hope you have found these to be helpful, thought-provoking, challenging, and most of all, encouraging. I recommend that you start over and go through these all again to see how you are doing.

I leave you with one last verse as a takeaway from Ephesians 4:1-3, "I therefore, a prisoner for the Lord, urge you to walk in a manner worthy of the calling to which you have been called, with all humility and gentleness, with patience, bearing with one another in love, eager to maintain the unity of the Spirit in the bond of peace." Now, go out there and be an influencer for Jesus.

Live honorably, love completely, and choose wisely – develop an eternal perspective and choose to finish well. May God richly bless you as you live your life from now on, making wise choices daily.

Author's Note:

When I was a college freshmen, I was introduced to the Fruit of the Spirit (found in Galatians 5:22-23) and it changed my life as I was led to make those attributes a benchmark and foundation for my life. I built on those by adding others to my collection as I became aware of them. I hate to think where I would be today if I had not discovered these character traits and made them foundational to my faith.

These are not just for adults. The younger one is who discovers the power of learning how to intentionally live out theses virtues, the more solid and prepared they will be to face the difficulties of this world in which we live and have the tools necessary to live a Christ-like life that honors and glorifies God—our ultimate goal as a Christ-follower.

Did this devotional series bless you? If you think this book would benefit others, would you be willing to go to Amazon and leave a review? We all rely so heavily on those, don't we—especially if we are unfamiliar with the author. It would be a way to support this ministry for free and would mean so much. Who knows, your review might even influence someone to change the course of their life and point them in the right direction—giving them hope for a brighter future walking more intimately with Christ. How exciting it would be to share in that!

If you are logged into your Amazon account you can just click on this link and it will take you to the page where you can leave a review. https://tinyurl.com/DevotionalReview

Be sure to check out my website: https://www.DebbySibert.com to get the latest information about all and my newest publications. There you also will find a contact form if you have any questions or concerns. In the "Author" section you can see the topics on which I am available to speak for women's groups at your church or para-church organization. If you follow DebbySibertAuthor on Facebook, you will receive my daily inspirational quotes.

God bless you on your journey,

Debby Sibert

Follow and connect with me on your favorite social media platform:
https://DebbySibert.com
https://twitter.com/debbysibert
https://www.linkedin.com/in/debsibert/
https://www.pinterest.com/debbysibert/
https://www.instagram.com/debbysibert/
https://www.facebook.com/DebbySibertAuthor

DO YOU WANT DEBBY'S *FREE* COMPANION BOOKLET?

Debby is always looking for ways to help her readers along in their spiritual journey. This particular giveaway complements this book with instructions on how to get the ability and resources to carry out the advice given for making wise choices. The companion booklet, a sixteen-page pdf, is a perfect follow-up titled, *Thriving in the Vine.* It's a study of what it's like to receive power and nourishment as a branch connected to the "Vine of Life" taken from John 15.

If you'd like to receive this free eBook and to be notified when she's launching any new free or paid books, please consider signing up at the following link. In fact, those who sign up will be the first to be notified when new books are available for purchase as well.

Whenever she launces a book, it is highly discounted at launch.

Check out this free booklet and download it for free here: https://tinyurl.com/ThrivingVine

Or use this **QR** code to access it.

APPENDIX
Attributes of God

This list is not exhaustive but contains plenty of God's attributes to blow the human mind about God's unfathomable character. I could quote dozens of verses to back up each attribute of God listed here, but I picked one for each to help if you would like to expand your knowledge and understanding of each.

Accessible – He lives in every believer, and we can access Him at any time. (Galatians 2:20)

Compassionate – The outpouring of Christ's blood to make grace available to all of us reflects God's compassionate heart. (Psalm 103:13)

Creator – No one Created God. There never was a time when He did not exist. Only He can bring something out of nothing, and He created everything. The same God who created the entire universe and all its galaxies created, loves, and knows you by name! He created us all for a special purpose. (Genesis 1)

Eternal – He always was and always will be. He exists outside the boundary of space and time. Because He is eternal, He offers us eternal life with Him, which He alone can give. (Romans 1:20)

Faithful – We can always trust Him in all things and to keep His promises. This is the basis of our confidence in Him. He can never *not* be faithful as that is part of His divine nature and would require Him to change. He cannot cease to be who He is. (Deuteronomy 7:9)

Father – He is Father only to those who believe in His Son, Jesus Christ. We are all His creation, but we are only His children if we are willing to call Him Father. He lovingly protects, cares for, and disciplines His children. He longs for an intimate relationship with us. (John 14:23)

Forgiving – Forgiveness is an outpouring of God's love. None deserve it, yet God offers it freely to all who accept the substitutionary, sacrificial death of Jesus Christ on the cross. (1 John 1:9)

Glorious – God's glory exhibits the total of all His many attributes. He is infinitely beautiful and magnificent, full of grace and mercy. The Lord Jesus reveals God's glory completely. His radiance and beauty emanate from all that He is and does. Our whole existence and purpose are to glorify and bring glory to Him. (Psalm 19:1)

Good – He is infinitely, unchangingly kind and full of hope and goodwill. We see God's goodness in His love and faithfulness. Even when bad things happen, God always promises to make all things work together for good. (Romans 8:28)

Gracious – Grace is God's kindness and favor to all of us who do not deserve it. He is slow to anger and great in lovingkindness. Grace is so much a part of God and so inextinguishable that He can no more hide it than the sun can hide its brightness. (Ephesians 2:8–9)

Guide – God is our light, illuming our path, guiding us in the way we should go. Without His direction, we would stumble and fall like those probing their way in the darkness. (Proverbs 3:5–6)

Healer – God is the great Physician and has the power to heal at will, miraculously, or through traditional methods. (Psalm 103:1–3)

Holy – God is high and lifted up and set apart above His creation. He is always perfect with a purity that is incapable of being anything other than what it is. Holy is the way God is, and He is the standard. He has set us apart to be holy as He is holy. Because He is holy, all His attributes are holy. (Isaiah 6:3)

Immutable – God and nothing about Him will ever change. He cannot change. While it is impossible for man *not* to change, it is impossible for God *to* change. He will never be more or less holy than He is right now. Because He never changes, we can always trust Him and His promises. (Hebrews 13:8)

Impartial – It does not matter your status, race, or reputation. God saves people, regardless of what they have done or will do. God will always do right by every person in every situation. (Romans 2:11)

Incomprehensible – We will never be able to understand God's thoughts and ways, which are much higher than ours. Because of His Word and His indwelling Spirit, we can understand all we need to know. (Isaiah 55:8–9)

Infinite – God is self-existing, without origin. He is Eternal with no beginning and no end. He always existed and always will. God's love and power have no limits. God, the Father, Son, and Spirit are all the same: infinite. (Revelation 22:13)

Invisible – Since God is a spirit, we cannot see Him. However, God has made Himself visible through the person of Jesus Christ. We can experience Jesus's presence through the Holy Spirit with us now, and when He returns, we will see Him as He is, face to face. (Colossians 1:15)

Jealous – God's jealousy is far different than human jealousy. His is one of protective love. He is righteously angry when His children choose to devote their time and attention to lesser things. Out of His love for us, when we turn our back on Him, He pursues us with all that He has. (Exodus 34:14)

Joy – Just like God is love and truth, He also is joy. Our joy is rooted in who God is. We can experience internal joy no matter what our circumstances because God reigns. (Nehemiah 8:10)

Just – God's justice is unchangeably right and perfect. His decisions are always a reflection of His righteous character. Because He is holy, He cannot ignore sin. But, because He is just, God will never punish His children who have put their trust in Him, accepting the sacrifice Jesus paid on the cross for our sins. (1 Corinthians 6:11)

Love – God has always been love. It's who He is. It is an essential attribute of God. If He stopped *loving*, He would have to stop *being*. His love never fails. The love of God is eternal, sovereign, unchanging, and infinite. God loves the world, and when we receive His Son as our Savior, then we have the capacity to love God and others with that save love. (1 John 4:16)

Merciful – Miraculously, God in His mercy does not give us what our sins deserve. He is unchangeably compassionate and kind. He forgives and restores those who humbly repent and turn to Him in believing faith. His mercies are new every morning. (Ephesians 2:4–5)

Omnipotent (all-powerful) – God has unlimited power, authority, and influence overall. He does all that He wills to do with no limits. Nothing can stop God or stand in the way of Him accomplishing His will. (Jeremiah 32:17)

Omnipresent (everywhere) – God is everywhere. There's nowhere in the universe where God is not present. There is no way to hide from God. Satan has restrictions and can only be in one place at a time, but God has the power to always be everywhere at all times. (Psalm 139)

Omniscient (all-knowing) – Nothing ever surprises God. He knows all there is to know. He possesses perfect knowledge and has no need to learn. He knows all our thoughts, words, and deeds. Only God knows all things, and we can trust Him to judge perfectly. (Psalm 147:5)

Patient – God is patient – an attribute we would do well to learn. He could put an end to human rebellion immediately, but He loves His creation and does not wish for anyone to perish, so He allows time for repentance. He is slow to anger, but one day God will come to judge all people. (2 Peter 3:9)

Perfect – God is perfect and upright in everything He does and says. All His attributes, His revelation, His works, and His Judgments, are entirely free of fault or defect of any kind. Everything He is, does, or says is flawless and true, including His Word—the Scriptures. (Psalm 18:30)

Person – God is an actual person, not an idea or an impersonal force. We were made in His image, so like us, He has identity and personality. He is one being in three Persons, God, Son, and Holy Spirit, equal in essence, but each with their own function. All work together to accomplish our salvation. (John 5:26)

Preserver – When we become a Christ-follower, we can be assured that He will complete the work He began in us. There is nothing we can do to lose our salvation. He preserves us so that He can accomplish His will and purpose for us. (Philippians 1:6)

Provider – God provides whatever we need. He provides for our daily needs, as well as a way out of temptation, and protects us from evil. He is the great I AM, meaning He is ALL we could ever need. God's greatest gift to us is His Son. Because of that, we can trust Him to give us everything else we need. (1 Corinthians 10:13)

Righteous – We can count on God to be right in all He does. All His words, actions, and plans are always pure and right. God Has no sin, is perfect in every way, and certainly never lies. We can count on Him to be fair, just, and faithful in all He does. Because God is righteous, He expects us to be righteous as well. Even the best person cannot be perfectly righteous, but God sees His children through the blood of Christ that was shed for us and therefore clothed with the righteousness of Christ. (Isaiah 41:10)

Savior – Thankfully, God reaches down and rescue sinners from the penalty of death and hell that we deserve. Because we are dead in our sin, we have no power to save ourselves. God's plan from the beginning was to save His children from the penalty, power, and presence of sin. He sent Jesus to live the perfect life we could not live, and He died in our place for our sin, exchanging His life for ours. On the cross, Jesus paid the ransom for us, which satisfied God's wrath against our sin. That leaves no punishment for us, His children. Jesus saved His children from sin's power and gives us new desires and a unique ability to fight sin through the power of the Holy Spirit, which indwells the heart of every believer at conversion. (2 Corinthians 5:21)

Self-sufficient – God has no needs. Because of this, we can go to Him to satisfy all our needs. He can do immeasurably more than all we ask or imagine according to His power at work in us. (Romans 11:33–36)

Sovereign – God controls all things, at all times, and there's nothing outside of His control. What God plans happens. Nothing happens out of His authority, and not even Satan can stop or change God's plans. He is free to do whatever He wants. When God permits evil, we can trust that in His faithfulness and sovereignty, He has planned to use it for our good and for His glory. No one can keep God from accomplishing His plan because He alone has the power to do it. (Luke 1:37)

Transcendent – God is exalted far above the created universe, so far above, that human thought cannot even imagine it. We should be in total awe of Him. (Psalm 97:9)

Wise – God is not only all-knowing. But also He is full of perfect, unchanging wisdom. He always uses His knowledge to do exactly what is right. The idea that God is infinitely wise is at the root of all truth. God's Word is full of His wisdom. All wisdom comes from God. As a Christ-follower, we have access to the wisdom of God. How amazing is that! If we are to be truly wise, we must seek Him. (James 3:17)

OTHER BOOKS BY DEBBY SIBERT

God's Antidote for Depression, Anxiety or Fear

Learn How to Experience Peace and Joy During Adversity and Uncertain Times

Do you ever wonder, "Where is God" when going through challenging times? Does He seem distant, or even non-existent? *What is the biggest crisis you are experiencing right now?*

We are currently living in extraordinary times, causing much anxiety even for the strongest temperament. There are many reasons individuals experience fear, anxiety, and even depression, and our world seems to be growing more and more fearful every day. If we ever lived in an uncertain time with an unclear future and reason to fear it is now.

Fear is a natural response for humans and has its place to help keep us safe. However, living in fear is counter-productive and is not an option if we are going to get through any difficult circumstances. We cannot allow ourselves to get stuck there and dwell on these negative issues.

Believe it or not, there is a way to experience peace in the midst of all of this and that is what I will be unpacking in this book. We have many choices in life. Every day we're making more choices than we realize. Peace is another choice that we can make over fear and anxiety. It takes recognizing where our mind is going and living with the intention to make a U-turn and choosing peace.

In this book, we take a hard look at fear, anxiety, and depression—defining them, discussing the symptoms and causes of each, and how to overcome them. One cannot read this book without being changed from the inside out if the shared truths are taken seriously, acted upon, and allowed to permeate and become a reality in the reader's heart and mind.

I have learned the antidote to the fear and uncertainty that often leads to anxiety and depression. I want more than anything to share it with you because I am confident you can find relief for your souls through the message I believe the Lord has given me to share with you. *Available now on Amazon.*

* * * * * * * * * * * * * * *

Where Will You Spend Eternity
Not Sure? There's Still Time

If you do not yet know Christ and the reason you *must* have a relationship with Him, then you need to read my first book, *Where Will You Spend Eternity?* If you are not sure whether or not you're going to heaven when you die, this book is for you.

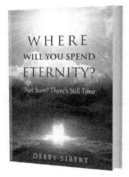

We live in a busy world, don't we? Do you find yourself living just in the present? Do you ever think much about or plan for the future—not just retirement, but beyond the grave?

What is your destiny? What will happen to you when you die? Do you know for certain where you're headed, or are you not quite sure? Do you even know how serious that question is? The Bible tells us that once we die, our body decays, but our spirit lives on forever. If that's true, and it is, then it's essential to know where you will spend eternity.

That's what this book is all about. You can positively know you will go to heaven, but not everyone gets to go there. The alternative destination is catastrophic, which you must avoid at all costs. It's essential to get that straightened out now while you're still alive and have the chance to change the trajectory of your life. If you let them, the truths in this book can truly change your life for eternity.

If you are a Christ-follower, you can join many others who have found this to be a great ministry tool in sharing the gospel with those you love, care about, and want to see in heaven! This is a short, quick read, and when taken to heart, it will change lives! **Available now on Amazon.**

* * * * * * * * * * * * * * * *

Living the Life Your Always Wanted

Experience Peace, Joy, Power and Perfect Love During Uncertain Times.

Does the life you are experiencing right now line up with what you know to be what God offers through the Scriptures? Do you ever feel lethargic and distant from God?

If you were to die today, would most people assume that you were going to heaven as they look at your lifestyle? What you seek is what you get. What are you seeking?

Do you lack peace or joy in your life— feeling stuck in your Christian walk? Do you find yourself wondering if there is more to the "abundant, victorious" life?

Too often, we settle for far less than what God wants to do in and through us. Do you sense that there may be more that God wants to do in and through you than you are currently experiencing?

The cornerstone of the extraordinarily victorious, transformed Christian life is a vital spiritual union with the risen Christ—available only through God's grace. When God created you, He created a masterpiece, and He has an exceptional plan and purpose for your life.

If you are not sure what that is, I hope to help you figure it out with the use of Scripture, referring to our "Life's Manual" (the Bible) as the foundation of that discovery. My second book, *Living the Life You Always Wanted,* will help you to learn how to experience an amazing, abundant, victorious life of peace, joy, power and perfect love.

Do you want to take your life experience to the next level? If our answer is "yes" to any of these questions, then this book is for you. **Available now on Amazon.**

COMING SOON:

Forever Is a Long Time to be Wrong
What Is Your Destiny?

This book, *Forever Is a Long Time to Be Wrong*, is for those who struggle to believe there is a God or the Bible is true and relevant. In  simple layman's terms, I help answer some hard questions, backed by thought-provoking evidence which I hope will challenge previous "preconceived" ideas about God, Creation, the resurrection, and the reliability of the Bible among other things.

Do you call yourself an atheist, agnostic, or a skeptic when it comes to God, Christianity, the reliability of the Bible, the validity of the resurrection, creation, and all those Christian buzz words? Maybe you're a "none"—someone who doesn't want to be associated with any religious belief.

Could it be that perhaps you have bought into a lie that all the above is false? Could it be you have accepted your parents' beliefs without doing your due diligence to research the truth for yourself?

Could it be you made a religious decision when you are a child based on what you knew at the time and are stuck there not giving it much thought now that you are older and more mature?

One thing we both can agree on is someday we will die. I'm telling you there are only two destinations—heaven and hell, and we don't just return to dust.

If you don't believe that, forever is a long time to be wrong. Once you leave this world, there is no chance to change your mind. It will be too late. The time to get that figured out and straightened out is now while you are still alive.

If you did not want to have anything to do with God while on this earth, He will not force you to spend eternity with Him. He will say, "*thy* will be done," and you will be separated from Him or anything good *forever.*

The purpose of this book is to help walk you through some difficult questions with reliable evidence that hopefully will convince you of the need to make a U-turn. We are not promised tomorrow, and every breath we take is a gift. Please don't put this off!

****

God's Toolbox for a Fulfilling Marriage
Learn What the Required Tools Are and How to Acquire Them

This book, for couples is forthcoming, *God's Toolbox for Marriage.* It is still in my head and my heart. I will get it in print as soon as I am able. My husband and I have been mentoring struggling married couples officially for over fifteen years, unofficially for decades. This is my passion because I know an amazing marriage is fully possible and am so sad that many couples never get to experience it, at least after the honeymoon period is over and reality sets in.

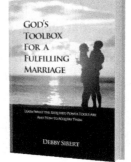

Any marriage help book is basically a toolbox of tips regarding how to get along with your spouse in the interest of having a successful marriage. Success looks different to different people, but it goes without saying and would be fair to conclude that we all want to be happy in our relationships.

A "Christian" marriage help book will go way beyond the typical psychology of "getting along." In this particular marriage manual, before the various tools for communication, conflict resolution, etc., are discussed, the content is focused on the foundational principles found in Scripture which teaches how to live lives of obedience and surrender to Christ which then gives us the ability to love and serve one another as Christ modeled.

There is no way we can have the ultimate marriage without having the guidance and direction of the Holy Spirit to empower us to love perfectly with the integrity and humility of Christ. It *IS* possible, and this book will give you the tools, encouragement, and instruction to achieve an amazing marriage that is the envy of all who know y

Made in the USA
Las Vegas, NV
28 May 2022

49472865R00095